When People
Are the Problem

Management Dilemmas

When facing a difficult management challenge, wouldn't it be great if you could turn to a panel of experts to help guide you to the right decision? Now you can, with books from the Management Dilemmas series. Drawn from the pages of *Harvard Business Review*, each insightful guide poses a range of familiar and perplexing business situations and shares the wisdom of a small group of leading experts on how each of them would resolve the problem. Engagingly written, these interactive, solutions-oriented collections allow readers to match wits with the experts. They are designed to help managers hone their instincts and problem-solving skills to make sound judgment calls on everyday management dilemmas.

Other books in the series

When Change Comes Undone

When Good People Behave Badly

When Marketing Becomes a Minefield

When Your Strategy Stalls

MANAGEMENT DILEMMAS

When People

Are the Problem

Harvard Business School Press

Boston, Massachusetts

The *Harvard Business Review* articles in this collection are available as individual reprints. Discounts apply to quantity purchases. For information and ordering please contact Customer Service, Harvard Business School Publishing, Boston, MA 02163. Telephone (617) 783-7500 or (800) 988-0886, 8 AM to 6 PM Eastern Time, Monday through Friday. Fax (617) 783-7555, 24 hours a day. E-mail: custserv@hbsp.harvard.edu

Library of Congress Cataloging-in-Publication Data
Management dilemmas : when people are the problem.
    p.   cm. — (Management dilemmas series)
    Includes index.
    ISBN 1-59139-713-8
1. Problem employees—Problems, exercises, etc.   2. Personnel management—Problems, exercises, etc.   3. Interpersonal relations—Problems, exercises, etc.   4. Supervision of employees—Problems, exercises, etc.
5. Conflict management—Problems, exercises, etc.   I. Harvard Business School.   II. Series: Management dilemmas.
HF5549.5.E42W3348 2005
658.3´045—dc22

                                          2004024791

CONTENTS

Losing It 149

Introduction

Henry Ford famously complained that every time he wanted to hire another pair of hands, he had to take a human being with them. It's a quote that managers can all appreciate because it's a reality they've all felt—that people, with all their passions and peculiarities, create the most vexing of management problems. If only organizational behavior could be as straightforward as an assembly line, or as clean as the business models outlined in our strategy binders.

Did we say passions and peculiarities? We should quickly add another "p" word to the mix: prejudices. For this is clearly one of the largest issues in human resources management today—the challenge of getting people with very different backgrounds and perspectives to work together productively.

The need for better approaches to managing diversity has arisen rather suddenly for most organizations. In fact, it's been a one-two punch. First, the basis of competition has changed. In a services-based economy in which unprecedented numbers of us are "knowledge workers," organizations must create environments in which people can inspire each other's thinking, learn from each other's experience, and leverage each other's efforts. But, as sociologist Robert Putnam has proved, that level of cooperation depends on having a foundation of social capital in place. And this is the follow-up punch: Between demographic shifts at home and expansion of operations abroad, organizations today have far more heterogeneous workforces. The shared cultural basis that might have facilitated easy collaboration does not exist. Managers in human resource roles are acutely aware of the distance between rhetoric and reality. We all like to believe our companies celebrate diversity, but in truth we're still working on mustering tolerance.

Case Work

Harvard Business Review has devoted much ink in its feature well to the topic of managing diversity. Back in 1968, Abram Collier urged readers (in "Business Leadership and a Creative Society") to nurture—not smooth over—the differences between individuals and groups in the interests of innovation. On the topic of gender diversity, standout articles include Sylvia Ann Hewlett's "Executive Women and the Myth of Having it All" (declared one of the best business stories of the year in 2002) and, most recently, Anna Fels's "Do Women Lack Ambition?" "Dear White Boss . . ." by Keith Caver and Ancella Livers was a breakthrough piece in exploring the perspective of minority managers. The list goes on.

But the thorniness of diversity management also makes it perfect material for *Harvard Business Review* case studies. The issues are nuanced, and even with the best of intentions managers land in downright dilemmas—situations in which they're damned if they do and damned if they don't.

Perhaps this is why the case study is the longest-standing and most popular department of the magazine. Appearing in the front of each issue, the case presents a compelling piece of fiction, then calls upon real-world experts to comment on it. Its appeal is certainly due in part to this engaging format. But there's also the nature of the subject matter. When HBR's editors consider a case for publication, we ask three key questions: (1) Is this a problem that many managers (in various industries) face? (2) Is it a problem that is important enough to be on the CEO's radar screen? And

(3) is it a problem that we don't already know how to solve? It's a tribute to the work of management scholars and practitioners that many business problems have become tractable. This isn't to say that the challenge in question—say, optimal manufacturing scheduling or dynamic pricing—is easy or inexpensive to overcome, but the theory and toolkit exist to address it. Where the conquests of management science begin to taper off is where the case study takes up. These are problems for which we do not yet have consensus on frameworks and techniques. Case studies are valuable to both veteran and novice managers because they are everyday problems that have yet to be wrestled to the ground.

Part of the Problem

Ready to dive in? The summaries below will give you a taste of the content you'll encounter. Read the cases in order, or begin with one that bears some resemblance to a problem you are facing currently. Each of them features a character whose sheer difference is making an impact. As you'll see, passion, peculiarity, and prejudice all come into play—and the stories share a common phenomenon. In an earlier volume, we pulled together examples of "good people behaving badly." (That in fact was the title of a collection that was published in 2003.) Here, most of the central characters are behaving just fine. It's the people around them who are making all the trouble.

Will She Fit In?

Certainly, in this first case by Joan Magretta, the woman at the center of the action is blameless. One of the few women partners in a management consulting firm, she has just had the unfortunate experience of having a client make a pass at her. And it's not just any client. It's the key contact at her company's single biggest account. But Susan Carter doesn't feel she can take the problem to her management. She owes her success to date, she feels, to her ability to "fit in" and not make her male colleagues uncomfortable. Telling about the incident would probably lead to her discreet removal from the account, which she doesn't want (no other project offers the same visibility or bonus potential). And longer term, the ramifications might be even more severe. "You can bet that this will come up every time they evaluate you or think about you for a new assignment," a friend counsels her. "It will never be raised explicitly, but it will always be there at some level."

If you have any doubt that this case treads on sensitive ground, consider this: It's the first and only case in the history of HBR with a commentator who insists on anonymity. All we know is that she is the head of HR at a consumer products company, and a woman. And interestingly, she is the only commentator to advise Susan to keep her mouth shut. There's no question in her mind that Susan should try to bring about change in her organization to make it a place where women's ambitions aren't blocked by sexist attitudes. But this incident "is the wrong vehicle," she observes. The potential legal liability and confused emotional responses involved "would distract people from the core issue Susan wants to expose." The commentators advising Susan to go to management with the problem include Gillian Derbyshire (vice president and general manager of EZ Foil), Anthony P. D'Andrea, a director at Lucent Technologies, J. William Codinha, head of the litigation department at Boston law firm Peabody & Brown, and Freada Klein, a human resources management consultant. Together, the commentaries confirm how widespread the problem is—Freada Klein's commentary is especially damning of professional services firms—but offer practical recommendations for companies who want to create a more enlightened environment for all workers.

It Wasn't About Race. Or Was It?

Jeffrey Connor's case study portrays an organization that's splitting into two angry camps as a result of a minor incident between two valuable employees—one a black man, the other a white woman. Coming to work on a Sunday, the senior executive woman had swiped her pass card to gain access to the parking garage, and been surprised when another car pulled in directly behind her. Before proceeding down the ramp, she got out of her car and confronted the young black man at the wheel. He produced his ID, proving he was Dillon Johnson, an associate in the same accounting firm. She thanked him, drove in, and thought no more of it. But to him, it smacked of racial profiling, and he was offended enough to complain to the office managing partner.

Robin Ely of Harvard Business School notes that the organization's intense reaction to the incident suggests a culture rife with racial tension. She urges the managing partner to launch an investigation of how members of different racial and ethnic groups experience their work and relationships in the firm, and to share the results in the context of facilitated conversations amongst the staff. Diversity consultant Verna Myers advises him to establish a diversity task force to examine the company's policies and practices for any subtle biases. John Borgia, executive vice president of human resources at Seagram Company, suggests that he solicit Dillon Johnson's input in particular in outlining how the firm can become a better place to work. It can start, he notes, by being willing to drop clients who don't want to work with minority account representatives. Consultant Jeannette Millard believes it will take planning, companywide education, and changes in structure and staffing to transform an organization that has long-embedded prejudices into one that is actively inclusive. Her advice to the managing partner? "It is time to publicly address the existence of discrimination at Fuller Fenton, the need for change, and your own intent to lead the effort."

Oil and *Wasser*

As globalizing businesses engage in cross-border mergers and acquisitions, some of the most dangerous stereotypes they must combat are not about gender or race but about national origin. In this third case of the collection, by Byron Reimus, it's a British company and a German one combining in a so-called merger of equals to create the world's second largest food manufacturer. The charismatic chairman of the new entity tends to dismiss national culture differences as an issue, insisting that "food people are food people"—but the interactions we see between two counterparts, both heads of HR in their respective organizations, would indicate otherwise. When they fail to work together productively, is it because of true cultural differences, or merely perceived ones? Or is it more about differences in corporate culture or even a simple clash of personalities?

Professor Robert Bruner, of the Darden School of Business at the University of Virginia, begins his commentary by citing similar real-world cases like Volvo's and Renault's abortive merger, Sony's ill-fated acquisition of Columbia Pictures, and DaimlerChrysler's post-merger culture clashes. It's the chairman and CEO's job, he says, to present a new vision, a clear set of expectations, a solid operating style, and a culture that draws upon and respects traditions but rises above nationalism. But the two deputies could do their part, he notes, by going out for a beer. "A shoptalk-free evening in which Michael discovers more about who Dieter really is as a human being might go a long way toward melting away stereotypes." Leda Cosmides and John Tooby agree that national culture is a potent factor in human relations. Codirectors of the Center for Evolutionary Psychology at the University of California, Santa Barbara, they note that "the programs that create us-versus-them psychology are present in everyone and easy to activate." The best way to bring the organization together is to focus employees on a common enemy: the competition. Michael Pragnell, CEO of Syngenta, notes that the case company "has my sympathies." Pragnell himself dealt with similar issues when his company was formed from the agribusinesses of AstraZeneca and Novartis, and he shares the lessons he learned. In particular, he chides the CEO of the case for "failing to set a clear strategy and articulate a new value system before setting people loose on various projects." Finally, David Schweiger, consultant and author of *M&A Integration: A Framework for Executives and Managers,* argues for an integration transition structure and a clear stakeholder communication plan. There's a lot more going on here than cultural misunderstanding. The CEO, he admits, can't force the two HR heads to get along, but he can help them "recognize that they can either hang together or hang separately."

Mommy-Track Backlash

"Please don't tell me that I need to have a baby to have this time off." So starts this case study by Alden Hayashi, in which colleagues of a working mother have come to resent the allowances the company makes for her. Megan Flood is the mother in question, and her arrangement—negotiated when she was hired—involves a four-day work week with a commensurate difference in pay. Her coworkers have noted, however, that in practice Megan shoulders less than 80 percent of their workload, mainly because in light of her reduced availability, management does not assign her the most demanding clients. Now, two of her coworkers are asking for essentially the same deal, even though both are unmarried and childless. One wants to train for a major sports competition, the Ironman Triathlon, and the other declines to give a reason beyond a need for more personal time. It would compromise the organization's performance to have so many people on irregular schedules, but on what basis can their manager deny the requests for equal treatment?

None of the commentators on this case argued that parents, by virtue of being parents, deserve better workplace arrangements or effectively greater compensation. However, they differed in their approaches to judging the proposed flexible arrangements and defusing the growing tension in the group. Michele Darling, an HR executive at Prudential Insurance, advises the manager in the case to call a departmental meeting to tell people she is open to flexible work hours for everyone, regardless of their reasons for wanting them—but that each individual must make a strong business case for the change. She also notes that Jessica might encourage her eight account managers to think as a team, to devise a creative solution for balancing account coverage with personal needs. Chris Dineen, a software company executive, does not quite agree that all pleas for reduced hours should be considered equal. The reality of a client-serving group may be that only one or two such arrangements can be supported. Speculating that the new proposals are really a "form of protest," he advises looking for other ways to achieve fairness— perhaps by allowing people to bank overtime hours for additional time off. Author Elinor Burkett, known to be in the vanguard of a "mommy track backlash" to the extent it exists in societal discourse, presents the solution in the simplest terms: equal pay for equal work. She decries "the mess created by an ill-considered rush into family-friendly workplaces." Stewart Friedman, director of Ford's Leadership Development Center, takes that notion further by recommending a group meeting in which everyone speaks openly about their expectations in all areas of their lives. Embracing employees' diversity, he claims, means supporting their different passions. He advocates "total leadership," which integrates work, home, community, and self.

The Best of Intentions

The dilemma presented by John Humphreys in this case could be set in the context of any company dealing with diversity in client-serving roles. It shows a management team hesitant to place a minority employee in a position where he will be set up to fail. Steve Ripley, the African American at the center of the case, has the potential to go far in his career. He's the best of the recent crop of trainees in terms of product knowledge and selling skills. Cynthia Mitchell wants to snatch him up for her district and get him selling the company's investments and accounting services to her rural Arkansas farming customers. But her boss counsels her not to make the offer. He wants the company to have a better record developing minority managers, and the persistence of racism in the district, he believes, presents too many barriers. "I know it doesn't sound fair, and in one sense it isn't," he explains. But if Steve fails in his first assignment, it becomes extremely difficult to promote him."

Judging from the commentaries on this case, this is a managerial problem where there is one, obvious right answer—but the world doesn't seem to know it. The commentators agree that Cynthia should defy her boss's advice and make the offer to Steve, but acknowledge that the circumstances of the case are all too common. Harvard Business School professor David Thomas cites his own research in which successful minority professionals described pivotal moments in their careers. "It often happened when a client resisted being served by them—and their managers didn't hesitate to counter with, "This is our best person." Herman Morris, Jr., the African American CEO of Memphis Light, Gas & Water, has personal experience to report from his first job as a lawyer. "If a customer had any concerns because of my race, he or she got a very strong message from the senior partners: You retained the firm; every one of our lawyers is excellent and enjoys the full support of the firm." In a coauthored commentary, Daryl Koehn (University of St. Thomas Center for Business Ethics) and Alicia Leung (Hong Kong Baptist University) point out that the white male leadership of the case company might be plain wrong about Ripley's chances for success. They've seen the same kind of logic keep firms from placing women in international roles, whereas evidence suggests that "women tend to be better at learning the indirect style preferred in many parts of the world." Professor Glenn Loury of Boston University, the final commentator, notes ruefully that "You can't sue your customers." He notes the indication in the case that "poor performance in an early assignment means you'll never climb very high," and wonders if that couldn't be amended in this case.

The company, he believes, owes Steve some kind of assurance that it won't be a career killer if he does take the job.

Losing It

So far in this collection, we've explored organizational and client reactions to women in executive positions, people of color, and colleagues from other cultures. In this last case, by Diane Coutu, we consider another source of difference and dilemma: mental disability. Katharina Waldburg is "an original" and a rising star at the management consulting firm that employs her. But the case begins with colleagues noticing that her behavior has taken a bewildering turn. Privy to her thoughts (about, for instance, the obsolescence of language) and her private actions (like going days without sleep, churning out page after page of feverish output), we readers come to recognize that she is spiraling into madness. And when she proclaims to a CEO client that "God created the universe by giving it a letter," her managers know they must somehow intervene. But how?

Kay Redfield Jamison, a professor of psychiatry at Johns Hopkins University School of Medicine, recognizes in the case the clear symptoms of mania. Noting that a common tendency in such cases is litigiousness, she advises Katharina's managers to meticulously document all exchanges and actions involving her. And, given the prevalence of bipolar disorder in society, she urges all companies to develop general guidelines for handling psychiatric crises. David Meen, a former office manager and director at McKinsey & Company, believes the chairman of the case company has to put aside legal and business considerations and simply respond as a concerned human being—even to the extent of notifying Katharina's doctor or psychiatrist and asking for advice. Indeed, Norman Pearlstine, editor in chief of Time Inc., tells us he relied largely on his instincts when he dealt with a situation very like the one in the case—and that his instincts were probably greatly influenced by the fact that his father suffered from manic depression. "I promised her that no matter how long it took her to recover, she would have a job," he says, and "she told me years later . . . that my promise was instrumental in her recovery." The final commentary, by law professor Richard Primus of the University of Michigan, outlines the legal issues presented by the Americans with Disabilities Act. The company is entitled to fire her now, but might have a hard time proving that the reason was poor performance and not the disability. It's in the firm's interests, he concludes, to work with Katharina to identify a reasonable accommodation.

Part of the Solution

Six cases, six very challenging management situations. As the lead character in "Will She Fit In?" exclaims, "Talk about the things they never teach you in business school!" But is it likely, in your own management career, that you will face problems like these? Alas, all too likely. The logic of equal opportunities for achievement in the workplace is undeniable—it's vital to a business's health as well as society's. But long-established habits of mind will die hard. The American Institute for Managing Diversity, a nonprofit think tank, has presented the issue this way: "Tomorrow's challenge is not in the creation of diverse environments. These will evolve naturally from demographic changes. Tomorrow's challenge is anticipating, understanding, and managing the needs and issues that emerge from such environments."

Managing diversity will continue to be a problem area for business for a long time to come, with real change in the organization lagging the aspirations of leadership. At the same time, it's important to recognize that, in the broader scope of things, companies have been a force for positive change. Cynthia Estlund, a law professor at Columbia University, offers this perspective in her book *Working Together: How Workplace Bonds Strengthen a Diverse Democracy*: "At a time when communal ties in American society are increasingly frayed and segregation persists, the workplace is more than ever the site where Americans from different ethnic, religious, and racial backgrounds meet and forge serviceable and sometimes lasting bonds." According to her research, most people who have a close friend of another race made that friend through work. And those numbers are growing. In one survey, for instance, the percentage of respondents who reported having a friend of another race rose from 62 to 82 percent among blacks from 1964 to 1989, and from 18 to 66 percent among whites. In the context of pursuing a common, commercial goal, Estlund concludes, "People can be forced to get along—not without friction, but often with surprising success."

JOAN MAGRETTA

Will She Fit In?

Executive Summary

Susan Carter, a partner at a prestigious strategy consulting firm, is caught in a dilemma she never expected: her firm's most important client has made an unwanted sexual advance toward her. As a friend of Susan's observes afterward, "The easy part was saying no. The hard part will be picking up the pieces."

Susan is a savvy, successful professional who has spent the 12 years since business school climbing the corporate ladder. But this event throws her off balance, forcing her to confront some of the most subtle issues of power and inclusion at the highest levels of her organization. Her story takes us beyond the legal issue of sexual harassment to explore how gender can influence who is—and isn't—welcome at the top.

Executive Summary

Susan worries that reporting the incident will hurt her career, giving her a reputation as one of "those women"—the type that make men "uncomfortable." Throughout her career, she has seen women lose assignments because of that vague criticism. At the same time, she is deeply committed to making her organization an equitable place, where women are respected and valued members of the team. In essence, Susan desperately wants to find a way to break the unwritten rules and reform the unspoken attitudes that restrict many women's careers—without committing career suicide of her own. Can she do so and still fit in? Or is this one of those situations that are simply too hot to handle, for Susan and for her company? Three managers, a lawyer, and an expert on gender equity in the workplace offer Susan advice in this fictitious case study.

"And then, well, he just lunged at me."

"He did *what*?" Nancy asked incredulously.

"He lunged at me," Susan replied. "One minute we're sitting on the couch in his hotel room, rehearsing his board presentation, and the next minute he lurches toward me, knocking me over. I just couldn't believe it."

"Wow." There was silence on the phone line.

"Yeah, wow," Susan repeated. "Now what do I do?"

Susan Carter was a partner at the Crowne Group, a strategy consulting firm based in New York. Her good friend Nancy Richfield was an investment banker. In the 12 years since they had graduated from business school, the two women had kept in touch, often seeking advice and support from each other at difficult moments in their careers. Susan and Nancy were among a handful of women who had "joined the club"—attaining the rank of partner at elite, privately held firms in which 95% of the partners still were men. Crowne's New York office had the kind of partner mix typical of most consulting and investment-banking firms: there were 98 partners in all, 4 of them women.

Promotion to partner four years earlier was a goal Susan had worked hard to achieve. And her successes on the Pellmore account had given her a lot of visibility in the firm. In particular, her work with Brian Hanson, a group senior vice president at Pellmore Industries, was responsible for the dramatic turnaround of a troubled business. The turnaround had made Brian look like a hero, and he was so pleased that he had begun to champion Crowne to other executives at Pellmore. Almost overnight, Pellmore became Crowne's largest and most profitable client. Billings mushroomed to $28 million—more than 20% of the New York office's revenue. And Crowne's senior partners were hoping to expand the Pellmore budget even further during the annual account review the following month.

Susan could feel the tension in the back of her neck.

"So then what happened, after he lunged at you?" Nancy asked.

"I pushed him aside, jumped up off the couch, and said, 'This is not a good idea,' " Susan replied. "And— can you believe this?—*I'm* the one who picked up the slides, which by now were scattered all over the floor. Then I just got the hell out of there. I still can't believe Brian Hanson would pull a stunt like this. I've worked so hard. How am I going to get past this with him? Talk about the things they never teach you in business school!"

Susan's second line began to ring. She paused briefly, hoping her assistant would pick up. No luck. "Nancy, I've got to run now," she said. "Can we have lunch tomorrow? I really need some advice."

"Sure. I'll come by your office around noon."

Susan hit the button for her second line. "Susan Carter."

"Susan, it's Justin." The line was crackling with static. "I'm on a plane to Chicago, but I wanted an update on your meeting last night with Brian Hanson."

Just what I need right now, thought Susan. Justin Peale was the senior partner in charge of the Pellmore relationship. Tall, good-looking, and athletic, Justin was one of Crowne's leading rainmakers. The absolute confidence he projected to clients gave them the sense that no hill was too tough to take. But within Crowne, Justin had a different reputation. His colleagues respected him, however grudgingly, for his effectiveness in selling business. But those who worked for him directly could see that underneath all the bravado, Justin was basically insecure. In fact, none of the junior vice presidents liked working for him. He was good at taking credit for work others did and even better at distancing himself when things went badly.

"Oh, Justin, I'm pressed for time right now," Susan said, stalling. The last thing she wanted at the moment was to talk to Justin. "I'm off to Boston for a recruiting presentation. Then there's the reception and dinner. It'll be a late night."

"Well, when can we talk?" Justin persisted.

"Not until tomorrow afternoon."

"Okay. My office at 2?"

"Okay," Susan replied, relieved to have bought herself at least a day.

"Two o'clock, then!" Justin always had to have the last word.

Hanging up the phone, Susan stared out the window of her thirty-ninth-floor office at the Manhattan skyline. She knew that Justin hadn't been wildly enthusiastic about her being assigned to Pellmore two years earlier. At the time, Linda Bushnell, the administrative vice president responsible for client assignments, had pulled her aside. They had worked well with each other for years, and Linda wanted to give Susan a "heads up."

According to Linda, Justin was careful to tell her that he himself had "enormous respect" for Susan. "But we've got to do what's right for the client," he said. "They're a pretty tough bunch. I just don't know if the guys at Pellmore will be comfortable with her. Will she fit in? Susan doesn't feel like the right choice to me."

In the end, Justin was overruled by John McMullin, the managing director of Crowne's New York office. Susan had been a loyal trouper for Crowne, and John had promised her the next high-potential assignment to come along. He had kept his word.

John's okay, Susan thought now. And Crowne *is* a great firm. But the truth was that she and Nancy had heard some version of Justin's comments so many times during the years since business school that they had invented a name for it: the Comfort Syndrome. The two friends knew dozens of talented women—in their own firms and in client organizations—who had been passed over for the same reason Justin had tried to use to keep Susan off the Pellmore account: "We're just not comfortable with her." Or "We're not sure it's a good fit."

And it wasn't the first time Susan had encountered the syndrome herself, either. When she first joined Crowne, for instance, there had been some question about whether a client in the steel industry would be "comfortable" with her. The guys at the client were "very rough," the argument went. Would she be able to "bond" with them? Despite this concern, Susan was given the job, and the client ended up being tremendously impressed with the results of the project.

Why is it, Susan wondered, that we're never uncomfortable with *him*? Not once in her four years on Crowne's promotion committee had she heard *that* phrase. *Comfort* was obviously some kind of code, but what exactly did it mean when people said they were "uncomfortable with her"? She's too aggressive? She's not one of us? Or what?

Susan was convinced that most men were totally unconscious of the Comfort Syndrome. Just the previous month, for example, one of her male colleagues, someone she liked a lot, called her for a reference on a woman she had once worked with. "A client of mine is considering her for a senior position. What do you think of her?" he had asked. Susan began to describe the woman's considerable accomplishments, but her colleague stopped her short.

"No," he said. "That's not it. They're nervous about whether they'll like working with her." He paused. "You know," he said, "it rhymes with *witch*."

Susan had been stunned, but she was careful not to show it. If I try to explain to him why that's offensive, she thought, I'll become one of those women he's uncomfortable with. Susan was reminded of something her father once said. He had been a fighter pilot and a

---

"If I tell Justin, he'll panic. He might have me taken off the client's account. And then I can kiss my bonus good-bye."

---

great supporter of Susan and her sister. "To be successful," he advised, "many women in your generation will have to learn to fly underneath the radar—to go undetected—in order to get along." This advice had always bothered Susan: she wanted to believe she could succeed by being herself. But the older she got, the more she came to understand what her father meant.

Returning her thoughts to the incident with Brian, Susan began to play out various scenarios in her mind.

Should I try, she wondered, to smooth things over with Brian? I could use Justin's help in thinking this through, but that means I'll have to tell him what happened. And if I do, he'll panic. He might have me taken off the client's account: he'd do anything to avoid putting Pellmore revenue at risk, and he knows Brian is the key contact there right now. If Brian is upset with us, forget about a budget increase. And if I'm "moved" to another client, I can kiss my bonus good-bye—and not just this year's. I've killed myself for the last two years earning credibility at Pellmore. I'm finally at the point where it's starting to pay off.

I know what Justin will think, Susan said to herself: This wouldn't have happened if we'd put Don Finley in instead of Susan. But maybe I'm just being paranoid. Didn't Justin tell me only last week that I deserve a lot of the credit for growing the Pellmore relationship? And hasn't he been kidding me for the last month about the beach house he thinks I should buy with this year's bonus? He couldn't possibly blame me for what happened!

Susan's door opened. It was her assistant. "You'd better get going or you'll miss your flight," she said.

On the shuttle back to New York that night, Susan couldn't stop thinking about the irony of the previous 24 hours: My client makes a pass at me. I don't trust my boss—or the firm—with the truth. And then I spend an evening with a group of eager M.B.A.

students telling them what a great place the Crowne Group is for women. What's wrong with this picture?

Susan's presentation at the business school had drawn a packed house. And there were a couple of really impressive candidates at dinner. This was a part of the job that Susan loved: working with talented young people. Crowne measured its recruiting success by the number of bids it won against archrival Spectra Consulting. And in the previous several years, Crowne had been gaining ground, especially among the strongest female candidates. Susan knew she had a lot to do with that success. Whenever there was a woman Crowne didn't want to lose, Susan was trotted out to win her over.

The sad thing, thought Susan wearily, is that Crowne is, in fact, one of the better firms for women. She closed her eyes. It had been a long day.

Susan and Nancy always ate at Café Soleil when they needed a quiet place to talk. After the waitress brought their salads, they picked up their conversation where they had left off the day before.

"Did you see it coming?" Nancy asked. "Had Brian been sort of coming on to you for a while?"

"No—not at all," Susan answered quickly. "I mean, I've been working closely with the guy for almost two years. We've had at least half a dozen meetings like this one in his hotel room to review work. I thought we had great rapport. Part of my job is to get clients to like me, to build relationships. But there was never anything flirtatious on either his part or mine."

"So you had no clue what he was up to?" Nancy asked.

"No," Susan said firmly, but then she paused. "There was one funny thing, though," she suddenly recalled. "I really didn't think anything of it at the time. But maybe—"

"What?" Nancy prompted her.

"It happened that night, before Brian and I went back to his room. We were at dinner with a bunch of people from Pellmore, and Brian's planning guy pulled me aside right afterward. He said he was really sorry that he wouldn't be able to sit in on the meeting later in Brian's room. What was odd was what he said next. He asked me, 'Are you okay with that?' I remember being thrown off balance slightly by his question. I mean, I knew the details of the presentation much better than he did, so it struck me as an odd thing to say since there didn't seem to be much reason for him to be there in the first place." Susan looked at Nancy, perplexed.

"Do you suppose the planning guy knew something I didn't know about Brian?" she asked. "Do you think he's got some kind of reputation?"

Nancy shrugged. The comment left her wondering, too.

Susan pushed her plate aside. "It's not as though I haven't been in meetings with clients in their hotel rooms—it happens all the time in this business," she went on. "You're always on the road, you work crazy hours, and a lot of business gets done over dinner and sometimes late into the night."

"Yeah, but try telling that to Justin," Nancy broke in, "and he'll want to know what you were wearing. And, worse, maybe he'll start to think your success at Pellmore has been based on—"

"Don't even say it," Susan interrupted her friend.

"Okay, but don't be naïve, Susan. You tell Justin, and whether or not he pulls you off Pellmore, you can bet that this will come up every time they evaluate you or think about you for a new assignment. It may never be raised explicitly, but it will always be there at some level."

"I think you're right," said Susan. "The old Comfort Syndrome rears its ugly head. And this time, it's about me."

Susan's thoughts jumped to the upcoming account review. "On the other hand," she continued, "if I don't tell Justin what happened and our budget gets trashed because Brian's mad at me, I'll be blamed." Susan stopped. She was getting ahead of herself.

"You know what?" she said after a moment. "Isn't there a bigger issue here? We both know that most of the men we work with wouldn't do what Brian did. They would think it was wrong. And from everything I know about Pellmore's CEO, this is absolutely not the kind of behavior he'd tolerate. It goes beyond the fear of lawsuits: he's a decent guy, he has two daughters in college, and he wants to make a difference."

"Finished?" asked the waitress as she began clearing the dishes. Susan and Nancy both signaled that they were done.

"But maybe," Nancy suggested, "Pellmore *ought* to be more concerned about lawsuits. I'll bet you a million dollars that this isn't the first time Brian has tried something like this. Maybe the CEO really needs to put a stop to this guy."

"Maybe," said Susan. "How can he—how can anyone—be an effective leader when we all maintain this conspiracy of silence? When we pretend everything is fine? Maybe the same goes for Crowne. Maybe John McMullin ought to know, too."

"What do you mean?"

"Well, most of the guys on our executive committee—except Justin—are okay. They just don't always see the connections. I'm not trying to be a saint here, and I can't picture myself ever saying anything about this to John, but I wish there were some way to manage this so that something positive could come out of it."

"Or maybe it's simply too hot to handle," Nancy said. "You're right. Most guys are not like Brian. But a lot of them would say, What's the big deal? Get over it. They don't understand that the easy part is saying no. The hard part is picking up the pieces afterward."

Susan looked at her watch. "It's 1:45," she said. "I'd better run. It's time for my meeting with Justin, and you know how he hates to be kept waiting."

Should Susan Report the Incident or Pretend It Never Happened?

Five commentators offer advice on how to handle sexual harassment at work.

➤ Gillian Derbyshire

Gillian Derbyshire is vice president and general manager of EZ Foil, a specialty-packaging business of Tenneco Packaging in Evanston, Illinois.

On one level, Susan Carter's dilemma is straightforward. We all have problems with clients or customers at one time or another. When that happens, there is an obvious and normal response: you assemble the client team and you figure out an action plan to resolve the problem.

Suppose, for example, that the Crowne consultants had done some analysis for Pellmore and that the numbers did not make Brian Hanson look good. Brian might ask the consultants to position the data in as positive a light as possible during their meeting with Pellmore's leaders. That probably wouldn't be a big problem for Crowne. The partner in charge could easily respond with integrity, "We'll position the numbers as positively as possible under the circumstances."

But suppose Brian asked the consultants to change the numbers in a materially misleading way. That would be a major problem. And it's the kind of problem the partner in charge would be unwise to handle on her own. Better to take it to her colleagues. In such a case, would Susan be held responsible for the client's behavior? If the firm's leaders have any traditional core values to speak of, I doubt it. More likely, Crowne's leadership team would stand behind Susan and refuse to yield to the client's unethical request.

Following this logic, then, Susan should take the Brian Hanson case to her partners. It's a business problem. Treat it like any other. As for Brian himself, Susan has at least two choices on how to deal with him. One is to press forward as if nothing happened (the What's the big deal? approach) and see if he takes the escape route quietly. After all, he, too, has something to lose by having the incident exposed. Or she could talk to him and try to salvage the situation gracefully: "I must say, you took me by surprise the other night. I'm happy to put this behind us if you are."

But, having made the case for treating the Brian Hanson incident like a straightforward business problem, one has to acknowledge that Susan's situation strikes a deeper, far more troubling chord. Clearly, it doesn't feel like a normal business problem to either Susan or her close friend Nancy Richfield. Both women have achieved all the visible manifestations of success. Susan is a partner at Crowne—an elected member of the firm's leadership. Many regard her as a role model, especially the younger female associates. But, as many women in Susan's position discover, success feels qualified—conditional.

Susan's ambivalence reminds me of a survey of senior-level business managers that I heard about recently. The male respondents generally reported that they felt "accepted" as leaders in their organizations. The women, on the other hand, reported that they felt merely "tolerated." Imagine what it must feel like for these women to step out on a limb—to challenge the status quo or to call attention to themselves in any way. Think about it. An individual who is merely tolerated is not in an empowered position that supports her taking a leadership role.

Susan's real dilemma is that, whether she likes it or not, she must confront some fundamental issues about herself and the firm at which she has made her career. She has been asked by a client to do something totally unacceptable, and, as a result, she believes that an important piece of the business may be at risk. She obviously is afraid that she cannot count on her "partners." This is a moment of truth. If Susan is going to act as an accepted member of the team, she must bring the Brian Hanson incident to her firm's leadership.

But how? Susan correctly perceives that the Pellmore revenue is at risk and that her ability to manage the account may be compromised. It is unlikely, however, that Susan would be a partner at Crowne today had she not developed good relationships with some of her partners. Now is the time for her to use some of the equity she has built up over the years. She might approach John McMullin, for example, or another member of Crowne's executive committee who has supported her. Her objective should be a mature and sensible conversation about how to resolve the problem without compromising the Pellmore business.

But here's the bottom line: If Crowne treats Susan badly and blames her for what happened in the hotel room that night, then she has learned something important about the firm. On the other hand, if she already knows that the partnership will respond badly, then she also already knows that she is working only for the money. Although many women and minorities I have known find this bargain acceptable for a while, over time the price they must pay for living in "bad faith" becomes too high. They leave corporate America. Many join or launch small, usually entrepreneurial ventures in which biases and double standards, if they exist, can more easily be exposed and banished.

But they shouldn't have to leave. That's corporate America's great opportunity today: to create an honest environment in which diversity—defined in its broadest sense as diversity of thought and experience, as well as of race, gender, age, and so forth—is respected and valued. In such an environment, Susan's encounter with Brian *would* be a straightforward business problem. She would have nothing to fear in taking it public. This is the kind of culture that Susan's firm and others like it must cultivate if they want to retain the competitive advantage that diversity in the workforce can bring. For, in the final analysis, Susan's story is one about leadership, authenticity, and integrity—not only hers but also her organization's.

➢ Anthony P. D'Andrea

Anthony P. D'Andrea is capital accumulation plans director at Lucent Technologies in Morristown, New Jersey. He previously worked in the same capacity at AT&T.

Susan is between a rock and a hard place. She has succeeded in her career by doing all the right things and playing by the rules. She has understood the importance of not making men "uncomfortable" with her. But I think she's reached a point where all bets are off.

For once, making the men she works for uncomfortable is what she must do. Susan must tell Crowne's leaders about the Brian Hanson incident. If she doesn't, the underlying problem of the Comfort Syndrome will never get fixed. The question is, Will Susan be true to herself or is she such a slave to her paycheck that she won't risk the immediate consequences of speaking the truth?

Admittedly, the very fact that Susan has been placed in this position is an injustice. Why should she be the one to have to risk anything? But doing nothing is worse. If Susan allows this incident to pass without seeking redress, she'll never again be able to look a recruit in the eye. More important, she may have trouble looking *herself* in the eye. This challenge is not about the best way to play office politics. It's about who Susan is as a human being—it's about integrity.

Tactics do matter, however. Susan's boss on the Pellmore account, Justin Peale, has only one objective: keeping the revenues from the account flowing. He is a major impediment to getting the issue resolved. If Susan went to Justin, he'd probably cluck sympathetically and tell her what she wanted to hear. Then he'd do nothing. Or, just as bad, he might contact Crowne's managing director, John McMullin, and tell him the story. But it most likely would be filtered and full of innuendo.

Susan needs to be sure that the communication about what happened is absolutely clear. She should call a meeting with both Justin and John. The two men need to hear the same story, at the same time, directly from Susan. You can bet that Justin will squirm in his seat when this conversation takes place. And John won't like it much, either. But Susan's strategy will force them to take action.

Susan probably will have to ask to have herself removed from the client. That's another injustice, but it may be the only way she can continue to be effective at Crowne. What about Pellmore and its CEO? Susan is correct to ask how any leader can do the right thing if he doesn't know what's going on in his organization. Although her question is a good one, she shouldn't be the one to cross the line over to the client's camp. The repercussions would be too complex and too difficult to manage. John McMullin, however, seems like the right person to have a constructive conversation with Pellmore's CEO.

Susan should realize that she has more to offer her firm than it has to offer her. She's good at her job, and others have clearly recognized that. She has a real card to play—and this is the time to play it. Susan must be willing to walk away from Crowne, to work for a competing firm if necessary. She has to be determined, not hesitant. And she must be assertive. No one ever broke through the glass ceiling while cowering.

➤ Anonymous

This commentary was submitted under the condition of anonymity by the female vice president of human resources at a consumer products company.

My advice to Susan is, Don't get mad, get even. Does this mean she should file a lawsuit or try to get Brian fired? On the contrary. It means she should do nothing and live to fight another day.

Luckily, Susan is savvy enough to understand the complexities of the mess she's in. Brian Hanson has a problem: he's obviously not in control of his impulses. But, as people in Susan's position always discover, if she's not careful, *his* problem will quickly turn into *her* problem. In fact, it already has. The reason: Brian is the client—a male client. It's a client's world and a man's world. In other words, there is nothing Susan can do right now that will leave her better off than she was before Brian lunged at her. It's frustrating. It's not fair. But it's reality.

Should Susan file a suit or try to get Brian fired? No, she should do nothing and live to fight another day.

In reality, corporate America is filled with managers who resent and fear women and minorities, believing they are just lying in wait, ready to sue companies at the drop of a hat for harassment or discrimination. Susan's story is probably a lot more representative: a woman who is shocked and confused by what has happened to her. More important, she doesn't once mention the possibility of calling a lawyer. Susan seems to know business protocol well enough to know better. Legal action would get her little but a permanent unemployment check.

Still, Susan is understandably concerned about the larger social issues her problem raises. She has experienced firsthand the Comfort Syndrome—as she and her friend Nancy Richfield have dubbed it—which makes it hard for many women to succeed in their careers, especially when they near the top of the organization. So what should she do?

From what I've seen in my 20-year career, Susan will almost certainly get burned if she tries to take the matter public. Nancy is right to call such a strategy naïve. Yes, it would be good if everyone were aware of the attitudes that block women from moving up. But the Brian Hanson incident is the wrong vehicle; as Nancy rightly observes, it's too hot to handle. The potential legal liability around sexual harassment—and the fact that such cases always provoke deeply emotional reactions in an organization—would distract people from the core issue Susan wants to expose. Her boss, her firm, her client—all would feel that a gun was pointed at their heads. Under that kind of pressure, learning wouldn't take place.

In the final analysis, then, Susan has no choice but to back off. She should use the intelligence and intuition that have gotten her this far to know when the time is right to get people thinking about what they mean when they ask, Will she fit in? If this experience has truly awakened her to the realities of gender bias, then she should take that lesson to heart and keep up the good fight.

Ultimately, the kind of social change Susan is looking for will happen only when women make up a substantial proportion of the partnership—and of the ranks of senior executives in client organizations. That's the end she should work toward in order to avenge Brian's inappropriate advance. She should continue to lead her firm in hiring and retaining the kind of women who can help turn the tide. And while she's doing that, she need not feel as though she's compromising her integrity by overselling the firm to female recruits. There is nothing wrong with telling them,

"The Crowne Group is a great place in most respects, but it would be a better place with you here." It's the truth. Susan should appeal to the kind of recruits who will turn Crowne into a place where the Comfort Syndrome is a remnant of a distant past.

➤ J. William Codinha

J. William Codinha is head of the litigation department of the law firm Peabody & Brown in Boston, Massachusetts. He has defended several major companies in cases of alleged sexual harassment.

There can be zero tolerance in today's business environment for the type of conduct exhibited by Brian. It is not only boorish and crude but unlawful: "unpermitted touching" is considered assault and battery under most state laws.

Susan may choose to deal with Brian herself—by talking with him about the incident or by ignoring it. Either approach would likely prove ineffective. The first one could set in motion a chain of events that makes it appear as if she, rather than Brian, is the problem. For instance, having been confronted by Susan privately, Brian then might bring *his* version of events forward as a preemptive strike, forcing Susan to endure a public "trial" based on rumor and innuendo. No one wins in the ensuing mess: not Susan, not Crowne, not other women who have to deal with the Brian

Hansons of the world. By ignoring the situation, on the other hand, Susan may be encouraging Brian to try again— a result she surely doesn't intend.

Another option: Susan could take her case to the local police and file criminal assault-and-battery charges against Brian. This strategy also is unlikely to achieve a satisfactory resolution. Susan soon might become burdened with large legal fees to defend her allegations, as well as with a new reputation as an extremist or troublemaker.

What Susan *should* do is formally document and report the incident to authorities within both Crowne and Pellmore. From my experience, this strategy is the one that ultimately will work in her best interest.

Most companies the size of Crowne have sexual harassment policies in effect. Susan should review Crowne's policy to see whether it addresses sexual harassment of employees by clients. She also should check whether its protection extends to partners. From a legal and ethical point of view, it should; but there are some firms in which partners, as owners, receive only limited protection.

Very soon after Susan reviews the policy, she should let the chairman of Crowne's executive committee know about the incident. To delay is to risk giving Brian the opportunity to claim that Susan has "conjured the situation up" because, for example, of anticipated changes in Pellmore's business relationship with Crowne. The memo that Susan gives the chairman should describe the incident and list any witnesses to it, which in this case would include Brian's "planning guy" and Susan's friend Nancy. In her meeting with the chairman, Susan should request that he lodge a formal complaint with his counterpart at Pellmore.

When he lodges the complaint, the chairman of Crowne's executive committee should emphasize that the working relationship between Crowne and Pellmore is an important one and that Crowne wants it to continue. However, he must be clear that Crowne expects a response to the complaint. Brian should be sanctioned in some appropriate way. Interestingly, Pellmore might actually welcome the information about Brian because it could very well be in the process of building a case against him for other transgressions of this nature. Or the company may value the information simply so it can avoid putting Brian in situations where he might be able to make other unwanted approaches.

After Susan's meeting with Crowne's chairman, it may be politically wise for her to discuss the incident immediately with Justin. She should try to make an ally of him, although that may not be possible. Justin's predictable irritation with Susan may eventually be mitigated if it turns out—as it often does in such cases—that Brian has behaved similarly with other women both inside and outside his own company.

The easiest solution for Susan, of course, would be to pretend that the incident with Brian never happened. Reporting the problem will undoubtedly lead to some awkwardness, some uncomfortable meetings, and perhaps even some confrontations. But the easiest solution in this case is not the best. The law clearly upholds a woman's right to be protected from unwanted sexual attention and touching, and it requires companies to adopt policies and procedures to discourage and punish such behavior.

Susan has an obligation—to herself and to others—to use the protections that were enacted on her behalf. Pellmore has an obligation to deal appropriately with Brian. And Crowne—including Justin—has an obligation to do what is right by placing the protection of one of its members ahead of any particular piece of business, no matter how profitable.

➤ Freada Klein

Freada Klein is a principal of Klein Associates, an organizational development and human resources consulting firm in Boston, Massachusetts. She has been working on issues of discrimination and diversity since the early 1970s.

Susan is in a no-win situation. If she speaks out, she's sure to damage her career. If she stays silent, she damages her sense of personal integrity, not to mention the cause of the millions of working women who do daily battle with subtle and overt forms of sexual harassment. But it's hard to ask a blameless person to be a martyr. Susan shouldn't have to pay the price for Brian's behavior, although she will no matter what course of action she takes. In fact, the only upside of this sad case is what it teaches us about the Crowne Group: that it is an excellent example of how not to manage gender issues.

The fact that Susan feels trapped in her dilemma and solicits counsel from a friend outside her firm suggests that Crowne, like many other professional-services firms, has paid little attention to gender issues that may arise when employees conduct business with clients. Our surveys of such firms show that approximately one-third of female partners report that they were subjected to unwanted sexual attention during the preceding year. The initiators of that behavior are almost evenly divided among male clients, male peers, and more senior male partners. The only way in which Susan's experience is unusual is that her harasser did not begin with verbal harassment before escalating his "pass" to a physical assault.

Professional-services firms that provide little assistance to women who have been subjected to unwelcome sexual attention usually share other characteristics as well. For instance, Crowne's human resources function probably handles support staff only; a partners' committee probably handles other personnel issues, mostly limited to recruiting, compensation, and election to partner. The firm undoubtedly has a policy on sexual harassment; most likely it is brief, it was designed for minimal compliance with the law, and it does not mention special circumstances, such as harassment initiated by clients or other third parties. The policy almost surely provides for only a formal grievance and investigation procedure, over which Susan would have no control once it was set in motion. The firm's leaders would decide whether she should remain with the client and whether she should ever again be assigned to a significant client. They would, in other words, set the limits of her career.

It's not surprising, then, that research indicates that firms like Crowne hear about only 5% to 10% of the situations in which partners or employees feel subjected to unwanted sexual attention. The other 95% share Susan's bind: ignore the incident or maneuver around it and hope it doesn't blow up.

Crowne is probably typical of professional-services firms in other ways as well. A few powerful senior partners have a habit of drinking too much at in-house functions and behaving inappropriately, especially with summer associates. Some senior partners have a reputation for habitually dating women junior to them. A handful are on their second or third marriages to substantially younger women whom they met in the firm. Most of these women have subsequently quit to stay home with young children. Team meetings and hallway chats are occasionally punctuated by partners' descriptions of female clients in canine terms (such as *dog* or *bitch*) or by comments about the appeal of their specific body parts. The few instances of sexual harassment that female employees complain about are handled with an eye to the relative value of the accused and the accuser to the firm; a few men have been warned, and several women have left with a check and a gag order.

Crowne's very small number of female partners are probably not, as a group, highly supportive of other women. If they are representative of female partners in other professional-services firms, probably only half are married (compared with more than 90% of the men). Some believe they have had to make tough choices in life and have little tolerance for the "whining" of younger women. Others, of course, see systematic bias against women—and people of color, lesbians, and gays—in how the firm recruits, staffs, evaluates, develops, and promotes people, as well as in clients' attitudes.

Susan's dilemma results not from one sociopathic client but from a web of subtle forces. There is no evil conspiracy at Crowne; most of the firm's partners are simply oblivious to the problem. The firm's success relies on rewarding a very narrow set of skills and values: it expects employees to show analytical and quantitative rigor, to be devoted to serving clients, and to define their own effectiveness solely in terms of their contribution to the clients' and the firm's bottom lines. The firm doesn't quantify the casualties or the costs to its people—the egregious treatment they might experience or the diminished quality of their individual and family lives. When employees leave, they are seen as people who didn't fit in or who weren't of sufficient caliber to succeed.

If Crowne is managing gender differences inadequately, what's better? How can any company create a more enlightened environment for its employees?

First, it should have in place a customized policy for handling situations such as the one Susan is in—one that fits the circumstances of its particular business. It should have informal as well as formal channels for solving problems and complaints. It should offer sensitivity training appropriate to the firm's different constituencies. It should have monitoring and sensing mechanisms, which might include examinations of patterns of inclusion and exclusion in client-firm team meetings, systematic and anonymous surveys of employees on their experiences and perceptions relating to harassment and discrimination, and evaluations of partners—during formal performance reviews—on their sensitivity to these issues. Finally, the firm's senior partners should make an unequivocal commitment to apply the policy consistently—to make no exceptions, not even for rainmakers.

However, experience suggests that it takes a crisis to force a firm to act on issues of bias, harassment, and discrimination. Susan could choose to force that crisis. That's a personal decision. If she does decide to do so, she also should start putting together her résumé. And as she begins her next job search, she should screen prospective employers to determine not only the proportion of women who are partners but also the firms' *real* philosophies, policies, and practices.

Ironically, if Susan is edged out of Crowne, the firm may ultimately benefit from the "unpleasantness" she started. It will be forced to learn how to deal with gender issues fairly and effectively. In the years to come, good women like Susan won't have to leave. Good women will join the firm, and the bottom line will be the stronger for it. Too bad Susan won't be around to reap the rewards.

Originally published in March–April 1997

Reprint 97208

JEFFREY C. CONNOR

It Wasn't About Race.

Or Was It?

Executive Summary

Hope Barrows, a partner at the national accounting firm Fuller Fenton, drove to the office on Sunday and swiped her access card to enter the parking garage. She noticed that another car followed her in—without using an access card. Hope could see that the driver was a man, but she didn't recognize him. Concerned for her safety, she got out and asked to see his ID.

Dillon Johnson, an associate at the same firm, was rushing to meet a colleague to review a client's file. Seeing the garage door was open, he drove straight through. He was puzzled when the car in front of him stopped. The female driver got out of her car, walked over to him, and asked for his ID. He felt he was being unfairly questioned because he was black. Hope was white.

Now it's Monday, and managing partner Jack Parsons is being deluged with calls. The company seems to be splitting into two angry camps. Some charge that the organization is racist; others are outraged that a woman was made to feel unsafe. One thing is clear: this incident is just the tip of the iceberg.

Jack would like to think that Fuller Fenton embraces diversity, but the experiences of Dillon and other African-Americans at the firm tell a very different story. In fact, Jack knows that Dillon was taken off a team for fear that the client—an old-line company in Texas—might object. Jack is trying to calm people down, but he doesn't know what his next step should be. Four commentators offer advice in this fictional case study.

Jack Parsons put the phone back on its cradle and pressed his fingers to his temples. This wasn't his first crisis as managing partner of the Northeast office of Fuller Fenton, a national accounting firm, but it was a doozy. That was his 11th phone call about what had happened the day before between Hope Barrows and Dillon Johnson, two hardworking, valuable members of the firm. And he was certain that the deluge was just beginning. Each caller had been very upset, and it was painfully clear that no one was willing to back down. The firm—or at least all the people under Jack's purview—seemed to be splitting into two angry camps.

He thought back to the first phone call he'd received, at 7:30 that morning, from an associate who had talked to Dillon the night before. "I always suspected this was a racist organization masquerading as a 'good' company," the caller railed at him. "I'm sick about this, and I'm telling you, so are a lot of other people. We won't work in a racist environment!"

The last call had been equally charged but on a different tack. The caller was a female partner whom Jack had known for years. "This had nothing to do with race. Nothing at all!" she practically shouted. "If a woman can't feel safe in the parking lot of her own company, that's pretty sad."

The story was really quite simple—the basic facts weren't in dispute. Hope, a partner at Fuller Fenton, had gone to the office Sunday afternoon to get a jump on the workweek, as she often did. When she arrived at the parking garage, she swiped her access card and the exterior door opened. As she drove up to the inner gate—the usual point of security during business hours, when the garage door was open—Dillon pulled in under the exterior door as it was closing. Hope stopped at the gate and, instead of swiping her card, got out of her car and walked over to Dillon. She asked who he was and whether he belonged in the building. Dillon told her he was an associate at Fuller Fenton. Hope asked to see his identification, and he showed her his card. Hope thanked him, went back to her car, and entered the garage. Hope was white. Dillon was black. Somehow the incident, as small as it seemed, had started a storm that was threatening to tear the company in two.

And it was only Monday afternoon. It certainly hadn't taken long for things to heat up. Jack pressed his fingers harder into his temples and let out a small groan. Dillon had been on the phone to him from San Francisco at 5 AM Pacific time. He had flown there the night before to meet with a client. He'd been up most of the night. He was angry—appalled. He said the incident, as far as he was concerned, was an indication that the firm was racially biased. Judging from the calls Jack had received, most of the firm's African-American partners and associates agreed.

Jack had asked Dillon to tell him exactly what happened. Dillon said he was working out at his health club when he got a call on his cell phone from a fellow associate, Shaun Daniels. The two had planned to meet at the office later that afternoon to review the file for Dillon's San Francisco client. Shaun asked if they could push up their meeting because he had to be somewhere at 4 PM. Dillon was grateful Shaun had agreed to meet with him on a Sunday, and he knew they had several hours of work to get through, so he rushed from the gym and drove to the office.

He pulled into the driveway of Fuller Fenton's garage behind a red Volvo. The car just seemed to be parked at the door. "I remember thinking, 'What's taking this person so long to swipe their card?'" he told Jack. "Then I thought, 'Where's my card?' and I started looking through the pile of clothes on the passenger seat for my wallet.

"Then the door opened, the Volvo went through, and I didn't even think; I just followed," Dillon continued. "Then the car stopped again. I thought, 'What is this?' and I tried to see who was in the car. I could see it was a woman, and she was looking at me in her rearview mirror. So I waved. And waited.

"She gets out of her car, comes over to me, and asks me if I work in the building. I say yes, and she asks me for my identification. I recognized her, you know—didn't know her name, but I'd seen her in the building.

"I was confused. I didn't know what the problem was. Then I realized that she thought I had slipped through the door behind her because I was some sort of criminal. I'm black; she's white. Most people at the company are white. Case closed, in her mind."

"What happened next?" Jack prompted.

"I told her my name," Dillon said. "I found my wallet and showed her my identification. But Jack, I have to tell you, at that moment, all I could think was that this wasn't the first time I'd been made to feel like an outsider at this company because I'm black. When I signed on, I heard a lot of talk about how Fuller Fenton was reinventing itself as an incredibly diverse, versatile organization. But my experience tells a different story.

"My first week here, one of the administrative assistants saw the wedding photo I have on my desk. She looked really surprised, and then she said, 'Your wife is very light skinned.'

"I laughed and said something like, 'Amy is white.' But the look I got? It was disapproving, almost like she was disgusted." Dillon's voice trailed off. Then he said, "I know I could cut her some slack. She's one of the older assistants, and she's been here a long time. But it stung. She hasn't talked to me directly since."

He was quiet for another moment. Jack waited. "That was the smallest incident," Dillon said. "After four months here, remember I was going to be on the team for that consumer goods company in Texas? I was put on and taken off within 48 hours. I found out—actually just last night, when I was venting to a colleague about this incident—that the partner heading the team was worried a black face would put the client off."

Jack shook his head; of course, Dillon couldn't see him, but he answered as if he had. "Jack, I know it's true. And maybe the guy had a point—that client is a very old-line kind of company. But still, if this company is serious about diversity, is that any way to behave? That's not the kind of company I thought I was joining. And it's certainly not the kind of company I'm going to keep working for."

Jack knew the last story was correct. In fact, he'd argued with the partner about the way Dillon was treated. And he'd hoped, at the time, that it would be just one of those things and that he could work to prevent it from happening again.

"I called four or five colleagues last night," Dillon continued. "I asked them if I was imagining this. They all said no. This time it can't just be water under the bridge, Jack."

Jack reassured Dillon as best he could. He told Dillon he was a valued employee and that he'd do some digging, that they would all work to resolve the situation.

As soon as he hung up the phone, he called Hope and left a message asking her to come see him.

"I tried to call you earlier," Hope said when she entered Jack's office. "I've heard a lot of rumors going around about what happened yesterday, and I have to tell you, I'm shocked—totally shocked. I didn't ask for Dillon Johnson's identification because he was *black*. I asked for it because I was freaked out that a man was following me into the garage—a man who didn't seem to have an access card of his own.

"I was only concerned for my own safety," she said. "He could have been white, or purple, for all I cared. I thought there was a good chance I was going to be robbed. Or raped. Asking for his identification was the fair thing to do."

Hope took a deep breath and told Jack the story from the beginning. She often came into the office on Sundays, she explained. She liked the quiet; she got a lot done. She knew that at least a few other people felt the same way. Occasionally she would see other cars in the lot, and sometimes she would see people coming or going.

But she didn't recognize Dillon's car, and she didn't recognize Dillon. "What was he thinking, Jack?" she asked, indignant. "I'm not the one who was insensitive here. Dillon Johnson was insensitive to me by 'piggybacking' behind me when I opened the garage door. Didn't he know that any woman would feel vulnerable, and potentially threatened, if any man—or anybody, truth be told—evaded security measures to follow her into a deserted garage? Why didn't he just wait the extra 15 seconds and use his own card?"

"You know, I really never should have gotten out of my car," she chided herself. "I should have just called security. But I was thinking, 'Better to confront him now than to put myself in possible jeopardy deep in the garage with no one else around.'

"To be honest with you, I was also thinking about two of my friends who have been mugged. One in a parking garage, the other on a subway platform. Neither was hurt. Well, my friend Alice strained her back trying to twist away from the subway mugger, but she got off easy, considering. And I was thinking about what my husband said to me, two years ago now, when I started coming in here on Sundays. He asked me if I was sure that it was safe to come in when the building was deserted. He asked me to carry my cell phone at all times."

Hope paused, then continued, smiling. "I laughed at my husband when he said that," she said. "He grew up in Manhattan." Her smile faded. "I did have my cell phone in my hand when I got out of the car," she said. "I had punched in 911, and my finger was on the send button.

"I didn't *recognize* him," she said again. "I didn't recognize his car. He was wearing a T-shirt. Not that that matters, really. No one dresses up here on Sundays.

Still, no one usually wears T-shirts, either. I did feel a little silly, at one point, before I got out of the car. I mean, I was telling myself that whoever it was was just coming in to work and had been too lazy to get out his card. But scared overruled silly.

"And in no way—no way—was I acting out of any racial prejudice. Come on, Jack, this guy has some personal chip on his shoulder, and he's putting all his baggage on me. I was *scared*, for God's sake."

Jack listened and, at the end of the meeting, told Hope he would think about what to do. It was clear, he said, that she and Dillon should sit down in the same room to discuss the issue. He would set up the meeting and get back to her. Meanwhile, he told her, he did see her point. Not to worry about that.

For the rest of the morning and early afternoon, Jack fielded angry calls. He also called the human resources department and set up a meeting with Hope, Dillon, himself, and the regional HR director for Wednesday morning at 10, as soon as Dillon returned from San Francisco.

He just hoped he could hold things together until then. He would, of course, continue to field calls and try to calm people down as best he could. But what else could he do? For that matter, what was he going to do at the meeting?

What Is Jack's Next Step?

Four commentators offer expert advice.

➤ Robin Ely

Robin Ely is a visiting associate professor at Harvard Business School in Boston, on leave from Columbia University's School of International and Public Affairs in New York.

Charges of racism and sexism can, and often do, clash. And all too often the upshot is something I call the Oppression Olympics—a competition over who has suffered the greater injury, the victim of racism or the victim of sexism.

Hope Barrows would not have been afraid but for her knowledge of the frequency with which violence is perpetrated by men against women. Dillon Johnson would not have been insulted but for his knowledge of the negative stereotypes that whites have been acculturated to hold about blacks, black men in particular. The problem is, it's virtually never productive to engage in a dispute that centers on whose concern has greater legitimacy.

That's why Jack Parsons needs to push any conversation between Hope and Dillon beyond the actual scene in the parking lot. He needs to acknowledge the underlying currents that made this incident so emotionally charged to help each understand the other's actions and reactions. But Jack should mostly focus on addressing the larger issue at hand.

It's clear that the incident in the parking lot is much larger than a conflict between two people. The other employees' reactions to the incident—their swift moves to accusation and defense—suggest an organizational culture

---

The incident in the parking lot is much larger than a conflict between two people. The other employees' reactions to the incident . . . suggest an organization rife with racial tension.

---

rife with racial tension. What's more, the firm's black and white partners have very different and apparently heretofore undiscussed perspectives on the role race plays in the firm. Jack needs to use this event as the catalyst for action on an organizational scale.

To do that, he must first meet with Hope and Dillon, making clear to them that he sees the incident as indicative of a larger problem within the firm and that he intends to address it as such. Then he should allow each to tell his or her story to the other, without interruption, including—

and this is very important—the historical context within which each experienced the event. For Hope, this would include her experience as a woman, with reasonable fears, based on known events, of violence perpetrated by men against women. For Dillon, it would include his experience as a black man, with reasonable concerns, based on his own and others' experiences, that white people might be acting on the negative stereotypes they often hold about black men. If Hope and Dillon can see each other's behavior as reasonable in the given context, they should be able to stop blaming and judging each other.

Next, Jack should implement an organizational intervention. It would begin with an investigation of how members of different racial and ethnic groups experience their work and relationships in the firm. Then there would be a set of facilitated conversations in which employees would learn the results of the investigation and discuss them within and across racial groups.

For the organizational effort to work, Jack and the other senior managers must make clear to employees that conversations about the role race (and for that matter, other cultural identities) plays in the firm are legitimate and encouraged. They should discuss publicly their own experiences and share what they have learned throughout the process. Finally, they should take every opportunity to tie these efforts to the work of the organization—to articulate how the learning that comes from, and facilitates, better race relations among employees creates a more effective workforce and advances the organization's mission.

Let me be clear about this organizational effort. The primary goal is not for white people to learn how to be more sensitive in interactions with their colleagues of color. Nor is it for people of color to learn how to be less sensitive to perceived slights so that they might be less likely to be derailed by them. Nor is it for Fuller Fenton to ensure that such events never occur again—though there may well be gains in all these areas. The goal is for all employees to learn how to discuss these events openly and constructively, with as little defensiveness, blame, and judgment as possible, when they *do* occur. Because in a culture such as ours, these kinds of events undoubtedly *will* occur, no matter how sensitized or desensitized people may become.

➤ Vernā Myers

Vernā Myers is the principal at Vernā Myers & Associates, a diversity management consultancy in Newton, Massachusetts, that specializes in professional service organizations.

Jack should be curious: why would a bright, hard-working, assimilated young African-American man risk angrily confronting the managing partner over an incident that seems fairly innocuous? Usually when people get to the point of speaking with the managing partner, something is really wrong.

Jack should realize that Hope's slight was the straw that broke Dillon's back. A series of small incidents, or "microgressions," can sometimes be as serious as larger, more blatant examples of bias. They create a sense of exclusion, foster isolation, make it difficult for people to fully commit to their organizations, and add psychological burdens that affect performance. Jack needs to address not only this incident but also the larger issues it raises.

The meeting on Wednesday should help Dillon and Hope understand the feelings, thoughts, and experiences that informed each other's actions. They don't need to agree about what happened, but they do need to be willing to see each other's side. (If Jack's HR person doesn't have experience facilitating racially charged discussions, he needs to bring in someone who does. A skilled facilitator will make sure that each tells his or her story without interruption or accusation.)

Hope needs to hear about the many times Dillon has felt humiliated because of his race and how this incident made him feel about his workplace. Dillon needs to tell her about being bumped off the Texas team. And Hope needs to tell Dillon about her girlfriends who have been mugged and her husband's concerns. He needs to hear how it feels to be a woman, alone and vulnerable. My guess is Hope will find it hard to even consider that some part of her reaction to Dillon may have been based on our society's racist messages about black men. A real solution depends on how willing each is to listen to the other and examine his or her own assumptions.

Beyond the meeting, Jack needs to assess the extent of the racial biases in his organization. He should start by speaking with Dillon and other African-Americans at the firm, saying something like: "I'm really disturbed by the things I've heard today. I want to believe that it's different here, but I want to know from you what it is like to work here."

Then he should assemble a racially mixed group of people from different functions and levels of the firm to take a good look at Fuller Fenton's policies and practices—large and small, formal and informal. Do they support or create (subtly or overtly) barriers to the recruitment, retention, and advancement of African-Americans and other people of color?

This diversity task force should suggest ways to change the culture, such as providing opportunities for people to discuss racial and other issues of difference honestly. The process will be successful only if Jack openly champions it as an issue vital to the firm's well-being and longevity.

There's no way that the firm will be able to wipe out racism or prevent every incident of insensitivity, but it should be able to build a system that is aligned with its commitment to diversity and that provides channels for reporting and resolving issues that do come up.

Of course, I can't be sure if Jack is up to the task. Is he willing to take risks, make the time, or allocate the resources necessary? Does he understand how racism operates on the interpersonal, institutional, and societal levels? His inaction with regard to the Texas team leads me to believe that he has blinders on, lacks the skill to address racial issues, or lacks the courage to confront them. If that is the case, my only comment to him is, "Jack, you say that you want a diverse and inclusive organization, but what are you willing to do to achieve it?"

One final note for Dillon. If Dillon senses that Jack's response to him is intended to smooth things over and stop there, he has a tough decision to make—stay with the devil he knows or move to the devil he doesn't. He will need to do his research well because despite their talk, very few large accounting firms employ more people of color or are better at diversity than Fuller Fenton. An African-American man is not expected to be there and that has to do with racism, but it is also a reality. Regardless of whether Dillon goes or stays, he will need to create a multiracial support network of peers and mentors who can help him succeed.

➤ John Borgia

John Borgia has been executive vice president of human resources at the Seagram Company for the past five years. Previously, he worked at Bristol-Myers Squibb for 25 years in various operations, finance, and human resource positions.

I wouldn't be surprised if Jack is thinking: "I wish Hope had had the presence of mind to say more than 'Thank you' after she checked Dillon's ID card. I wish she'd said something like, 'Oh, hi. Nice to meet you. I'm Hope. Sorry we had to meet like this; I got scared when I saw that someone had slipped in behind me instead of using their own card to get in. Let's get together for coffee sometime.' A few pleasantries would have defused this situation, and I wouldn't be sitting here in the middle of a hurricane."

I could understand that train of thought. I mean, the poor guy did just get blindsided with a Monday morning crisis. But what I *hope* Jack is thinking is: "Here's my chance to make a real difference. It's time for Fuller Fenton to embrace diversity—to take its place as a company that has broken free of its old traditions and prejudices. I'm going to use this crisis as a catalyst for change."

What am I talking about? Strategy. Dillon just learned he was bumped from a team because a partner had concerns that a client would be put off by the idea of working with a black man. Jack felt uncomfortable about that action at the time but didn't take a stand. Now he should. He should use what happened between Hope and Dillon as a starting point for reexamining the kinds of clients Fuller Fenton takes on and the work that it will and will not do.

It's one thing to say that you want to embrace diversity. It's quite another to deliver on that ideal. It would send a huge statement if Jack said publicly that Fuller Fenton won't insult its own people to please clients—even if that means losing clients. Imagine the impact if Jack said, "There are enough clients out there; we don't need that one."

I'm a big fan of resolving disputes one on one, with as little fanfare as possible. But I really don't think that Dillon and Hope have a dispute. That's why I don't think Jack should meet with both of them on Wednesday. I would much rather see Jack meet privately with Dillon. At the meeting, he should say: "Look, this incident is nothing. Hope was frightened, as any woman would be, when she saw someone bypass the appropriate security protocols and follow her car into the garage. But you have good reason to be angry about the larger issue." Then Jack should talk with Dillon about how Fuller Fenton is being run. And he should solicit Dillon's support in outlining how the firm can become a better organization and a better place to work. Jack can call Hope—either before or after his meeting with Dillon—and tell her what's going on and what's going to come of the incident. There's no need to involve her in this initial stage of his new initiative, though, unless she wants to get involved.

I work in New York City. We have detectors on every door here. A security breach is serious business. But for Fuller Fenton, the security breach is not the primary issue. The alleged dispute is a straw man. What's really important is how Jack Parsons intends to run his office, and the influence he can—and should—have over the kind of firm Fuller Fenton becomes.

➤ Jeanette Millard

Jeanette Millard is an organization development consultant in Boxborough, Massachusetts. Over the past decade, she has broadened her focus to include addressing the dynamics of racism, sexism, and heterosexism.

On this particular Monday morning, Jack Parsons is getting the education of a lifetime. He is seeing firsthand the effects of years of institutional complacence and organizational neglect. He is learning that racism is more than a series of interpersonal events; it is a system. If you are white, chances are you've been conditioned not to see it.

Jack certainly needs to respond to what happened between Hope and Dillon. But there's a lot more brewing at Fuller Fenton than a few disgruntled employees. Jack needs to exercise leadership and address the organizational pattern of racial discrimination on both the micro and macro levels.

I'll start on the micro level. Talking with upset employees is a good start—but if that's all Jack does, it will soon be perceived as collusion. Similarly, holding a meeting with Dillon and Hope is an important step. But watch out, Jack. If all you have to offer is a lame "I hear what you are both saying," you might do more damage than good.

Jack needs to understand that different things happened to Hope and Dillon, and thus different responses are called for. Hope's situation is pretty straightforward. She had a serious moment of concern about her safety, and Jack should look into the Sunday security system. Hope doesn't feel regularly at risk at Fuller Fenton—this was not one of a series of incidents for her at work. The security system now in place will, with some adjustments, work for Hope and others.

But what happened to Dillon was part of a larger pattern of discrimination—and this is where Jack must broaden his response. Jack has seen overt discrimination at Fuller Fenton. Indeed, he witnessed an egregious event in which Dillon's ability to do his job was directly and negatively affected by his race. Fuller Fenton put itself at risk in that situation; another employee might sue. Dillon's most recent experience has served as a spotlight, illuminating the accumulation of grievances among people of color at Fuller Fenton. The best way to respond to Dillon, and to the firm at large, then, is to acknowledge the larger picture and to make a sincere commitment to rectify the situation.

On the macro level, transforming an organization that has long-embedded prejudices into one that is actively inclusive takes planning, companywide education, and changes in structure and staffing. Jack may find the prospect of such an aggressive and thorough initiative daunting. But in an environment with a history of discrimination, moments like the exchange between Hope and Dillon are countless, and they fly like sparks into the tinderbox of a system that creates endless "incidents." The time and energy required for such an effort is a much better investment, and much more satisfying, than fighting fire after inevitable fire.

Returning to the micro level: Yes, Jack, start with that Wednesday meeting with Dillon and Hope. And yes, continue to talk with other employees—you can help them see the bigger picture. The only way to reconcile Hope and Dillon—and the other employees at Fuller Fenton who are now at odds—is to help each person see his or her colleagues as individuals as well as members of a group. Then they will better understand the other's experiences and responses. In the hurried, stressful moment in the parking lot, Hope and Dillon reacted primarily to the other person's membership in a dominant group: Hope knew—and drew on—the potential for male aggression; Dillon knew—and drew on—the reality of white dominance and the usual denial of that dominance. To understand Hope's reaction, Dillon and others at Fuller Fenton who are up in arms over this incident must understand a woman's fears and take them seriously. Conversely, Hope, as a well-intentioned white woman, may struggle with the notion of her white dominance (she has learned not to see it). Hope, and those who are siding with her, need to understand that there is more going on here than a chip on Dillon's shoulder, and that they are all a part of it.

But Jack, after these initial meetings, don't let smoothed feathers lull you into thinking that you can avoid the larger issue. It is time to publicly address the existence of discrimination at Fuller Fenton, the need for change, and your own intent to lead the effort. Addressing racism begins in earnest when white people stop insisting, "It wasn't about race!" It is time to look at the whole picture, not just the cause of the current sparks.

Originally published in September–October 2000

Reprint R00502

Oil and *Wasser*

Executive Summary

It was supposed to be an amicable "merger of equals," an example of European togetherness, a synergistic deal that would create the world's second-largest consumer foods company out of two former competitors. But the marriage of entrepreneurial powerhouse Royal Biscuit and the conservative, family-owned Edeling GmbH is beginning to look overly ambitious.

Integration planning is way behind schedule. Investors seem wary. But for Royal Biscuit HR head Michael Brighton, the most immediate problem is that he can't get his German counterpart, Dieter Wallach, to collaborate on a workable leadership development plan for the merged company's executives. And stockholders have been promised details of the new organizational structure, including a precise timetable, in less than a month. The CEO of the British company—and of the post-merger Royal Edeling—is furious.

It's partly a culture clash, but the problems may run deeper than that. The press is harping on details that counter the official merger-of-equals line. For instance seven of the ten seats on the new company's management board will be held by Royal Biscuit executives.

Will the clash of cultures undermine this cross-border merger? Commenting on the fictional case study are Robert F. Bruner, the executive director of the Batten Institute at the University of Virginia's Darden Graduate School of Business Administration in Charlottesville; Leda Cosmides and John Tooby, the codirectors of the Center for Evolutionary Psychology at the University of California, Santa Barbara; Michael Pragnell, the CEO and director of the board for the agribusiness firm Syngenta, based in Basel, Switzerland; and David Schweiger, the president of the Columbia, South Carolina–based management consulting firm Schweiger and Associates.

Michael Brighton felt as if he'd been slapped. His back stiffened into the cold leather chair as Sir John Callaghan, the temperamental chairman of the London-based Royal Biscuit Company, angrily brandished the memo. "There is no evidence the two of you collaborated on this leadership development plan!" he hollered, glaring at Brighton while his German counterpart, Dieter Wallach, stared stone-faced at the conference table.

"This is a disgrace," Callaghan said. "You've had over three months to put together a coherent program, not a mishmash of features culled from warmed-over HR presentations!" He slammed the memo on the table.

The conference room's glass doors rattled slightly. Anthony Miles, Royal Biscuit's head of marketing, overheard the commotion as he passed in the hallway. He raised his eyebrows and quickened his step.

Callaghan, a self-made billionaire who did not suffer fools gladly, was famous for his displays of temper. But Brighton had never been on the receiving end of his boss's fury, despite serving as Callaghan's head of HR for over five years. Brighton was inclined to place the blame on his German counterpart, from onetime competitor and now merger partner Edeling GmbH, for the lack of progress. Still, he kept his mouth shut. "If Dieter weren't such a stickler for process, we would have been a lot further along," he thought grimly.

To some outside observers, Callaghan's tantrum would have seemed like the inevitable result of an overly ambitious marriage of two proud firms. On January 30, accompanied by Edeling CEO Heinz Burkhardt, Callaghan had stepped proudly before packed conference rooms in London and Frankfurt to announce the merger. On one side of the deal was Royal Biscuit, an entrepreneurial powerhouse that had single-handedly transformed the British snack food business in ten short years. On the other was Munich-based Edeling, a family-owned, 120-year-old model employer and beloved German brand. The new company, Royal Edeling, would amicably blend the British and German organizations, creating the world's second-largest consumer foods business. It would be a "merger of equals," the top executives proclaimed, and a great example of European togetherness.

Callaghan would serve as the CEO of the new firm, headquartered in London, with Burkhardt becoming nonexecutive chairman of the supervisory board. Shares of the company would be listed for trading in both London and Frankfurt. Under German law, the new organization would be governed by a management board that kept an eye on operations and by a supervisory board that oversaw management and represented all the stakeholders.

On paper, at least, the deal made perfect sense. But the merger was proving more difficult than the leaders of either company had imagined, and it was already May. Integration planning was dreadfully behind schedule, and stockholders had been promised the details of the new organizational structure, including a precise timetable, by June 1. As far as Callaghan was concerned, the difficulty Brighton and Wallach were having merging the two firms' leadership development programs bordered on the ridiculous. He had bigger fish to fry. The press was being neither cooperative nor patient. The British and German governments had yet to sign off on the merger. And the final verdict of investors was anything but certain. The last thing he wanted to contend with was bickering between two HR lieutenants.

"The two of you are supposed to be part of the solution, not part of the problem," Callaghan snapped. "Beyond the fact that the success of the new company depends on your success in shaping excellent managers, you are leading an effort that has tremendous symbolic importance. Our high-potential managers have to see that, going forward, we are of one mind on what it takes to get ahead in this organization. And that advancement will be a question of proven merit, not politics."

"But sir," Brighton began weakly.

"No buts!" Callaghan shouted. "You have one week to come back with a program that is demonstrably better than the initiatives either of our companies had before. And don't bother submitting anything less, or . . ." He left the threat hanging in the air and abruptly exited the room.

On the way out, Wallach was the first to break the glum silence. "If we have learned anything from this, Michael," he said with what seemed to Brighton a self-righteous air, "it is that we will have to draw on some additional perspectives, beyond our own, to produce the plan."

"Didn't you hear him?" Brighton responded defensively. "He already perceives it as a dog's dinner. And in any case, we don't have any more time to collect opinions and juggle calendars, as you keep pushing for. Sir John is right. The consensus will come *after* we have designed a world-class program."

"He is certainly right to demand a higher-quality plan," Wallach replied. "But I don't see how we can devise that in a vacuum." He looked at his watch. "I must catch a plane back to Munich in two hours. Can we meet at my office the day after tomorrow, preferably first thing in the morning?"

"Yes, of course, but please understand that we've already had three meetings. The clock is ticking. We must make some decisions, and fast. If we could just come to agreement on a few of the major components, then I can quickly . . ."

"We have a proverb in Germany," Wallach interrupted. "'What's the use of running if you're not on the right road?'"

"In England, we have a saying of our own. 'Any port in a storm.'"

Why Can't They Be Like Us?

On the way back to his office, Brighton stopped to make himself tea in the kitchenette off the reception area. Moments later, Anthony Miles walked in.

"Did you see this?" asked the marketing executive, showing him a press clipping.

Brighton put on his reading glasses and peered at the article. It read:

> Royal Biscuit's incipient merger with German biscuit maker Edeling is among the largest in the food industry's history. Despite the assurances of top corporate executives, however, British workers are not impressed. According to some employees, who spoke on condition of anonymity, there is growing concern about job losses and changes that might threaten the company's hard-charging culture. A few self-described "Royal Biscuit Men" were particularly vocal in their anti-German sentiments.

Brighton sighed and removed his glasses. "I know about this. In fact, I spoke with one of these fellows recently." He quickly summarized what he had heard from Andrew McCabe, a quality assurance engineer at Royal Biscuit and an affable, trustworthy, and productive employee. Forty-nine years old and the father of two teenage daughters, McCabe had never attended university but had quickly risen to a supervisory position. "Andrew is apparently worried that he might be let go in favor of what he called 'some sausage-eater,'" Brighton said.

"You know, the same kind of stuff is coming out on the other side," Miles observed, citing stories his salespeople had spotted in the German press. In one, Edeling employees fretted about whether those brash types from Royal Biscuit would have any respect for Edeling's proud history. In another, a financial columnist made much of the fact that seven of the ten seats on the new company's management board would be held by Royal Biscuit executives and less than half of the positions on the supervisory board would go to representatives of Edeling stockholders, who had received a modest 10% premium for their shares. "The British will gobble up every last one of Edeling's cookies," the reporter lamented.

Back at his desk, Brighton scoured the lists that he and Wallach had exchanged of high-potential managers in various divisions. It was inevitable, he knew, that to honor the "merger of equals" intent, leadership assignments would be divided between the two firms' people more or less evenly. Some of the people he had seen come so far would now find Germans sitting squarely in their career paths. Still, they were luckier than their colleagues who hadn't been tagged as high potentials. Brighton mused bitterly about a few borderline candidates who hadn't quite made the cut. Undoubtedly they had more spark than anyone on the lower half of Wallach's list. The real challenge before him, he decided, was to design a program that could remake those plodding Germans in the image of his best leaders—though he could never express it to Wallach in those terms. Meanwhile, the prospect of the talent exodus he would witness over the next two years—and the dilution of the culture he had worked to build—was depressing, indeed.

Calling a Spade a Spade

On Wednesday evening, Brighton flew to Munich for another of his increasingly irritating meetings with Wallach. After landing, he went to an old hotel in the city center, where he slept fitfully in a small, stuffy room. The following morning, after a quick breakfast of strong coffee, cold cheese, and hard rolls, he hailed a taxi. The driver, of uncertain origin, seemed to speak only two words of English: yes and no. After the driver missed the autobahn exit, Brighton arrived at Edeling more than ten minutes late. Rushing through the lobby, he imagined Wallach making note of his tardiness in some thick book of black marks.

In contrast with Royal Biscuit's ultramodern home office, with its high-tech accoutrements, Edeling's bland headquarters suggested a no-nonsense firm determined to keep a low profile. In Wallach's office, a letter box was the only item on the immaculate desk. There were two uncomfortable chairs for visitors and several faded prints on the walls.

The Englishman tried to be patient as he underscored for Wallach—yet again—what had to be accomplished. Their mandate, he said, was to lay out a program that would give Royal Edeling a unique and sustained leadership advantage. The June 1 deadline was looming, so they would have to prepare at least a rudimentary presentation, he told the German. "So you and I should have the deliverable at least outlined by the end of today," he announced.

Wallach would have none of it. "Michael, I understand that there is time pressure. But we still have fundamental disagreements. You fail to appreciate that we are an old company, and our existing systems and procedures are the product of many years of learning. And I must remind you that the way Edeling conducts business has always been very successful."

Wallach went on to explain—in what seemed to Brighton painful detail—how Edeling worked to cultivate its future generations of leadership, starting with recruitment. The company had always been very careful in selecting people for even the most junior management positions. Qualified candidates had to demonstrate high academic achievement in the *Gymnasium* and university. After graduation, they had to show proof of a successful apprenticeship, complete with outstanding recommendations. During their first two years of service, they were required to attend management training courses at Edeling's in-house university, which, Wallach reminded Brighton, was considered "the model for the many corporate universities that have sprung up since." To be considered for promotion, managers were also expected to excel in a variety of posts, working with teams both inside and outside their areas of expertise. "I myself," Wallach pointed out, "started as an analyst in finance in Munich and was transferred to public affairs in New York before returning to manage benefits. So you see," he summarized, "developing top talent is a matter of identifying the best learners and giving them the benefit of expert instruction. Knowledge—even of what constitutes good leadership—becomes obsolete so quickly in this business that . . ."

"Yes, yes, I understand," Brighton said curtly, "but I know Callaghan, and he will insist that your program is much too insular." Royal Biscuit, he noted, had produced dynamic leaders by focusing on diversity of background and "action learning" in the field. "We recruit the best and brightest from the business schools *worldwide*"—he stressed the word—"but even more, the people we hire and promote have a certain attitude and style, if you will. They show creativity and entrepreneurial energy."

Rather than subject them to formal classes, Brighton explained, Royal Biscuit put these promising young managers in charge of teams. The ones who emerged with the most productive teams quickly rose through the ranks. "At the end of the day, leadership ability is more about emotional intelligence, energy, and cultural fit than anything else—and those are not traits that can

---

Michael Brighton shot back at his German counterpart: "Perhaps this is a Teutonic tendency, but you have a pessimistic view of human nature."

---

be instilled in a formal setting. That's why we don't want to waste time putting people in a classroom; we want their feet on the ground and running from the start." And in light of Royal Biscuit's past five years of double-digit growth, it was hard to argue with the wisdom of that approach, Brighton added with some defiance.

Wallach shook his head in frustration. "Michael, you are more than hinting that Edeling should abandon the best practices we have refined over many years. And for what? A program that treats leadership as an art—and therefore resists any objective assessment? We see the development of leadership as a science. And to be honest," he added gruffly, "I would have a hard time endorsing a program that seems designed to pit your 'best and brightest' against each other. What leader ultimately succeeds without learning to collaborate and gain consensus?"

"They do learn that, because it works in practice," Brighton shot back. "You want to know what a large part of the problem is? And perhaps this is not so much your fault as it is a Teutonic tendency, but you have a fundamentally pessimistic view of human nature. You don't trust people to see what is good and to gravitate toward it naturally. That's why everything comes down to a disciplined process for you, and sticking with prescribed steps."

Wallach's stern, surprised expression made Brighton wonder if he had been too harsh. On the other hand, perhaps calling a spade a spade was the only way to begin making progress.

Bitter Truths

Brighton was thirsty. The late-afternoon flight from Munich had been short but turbulent. His head hurt, and he was tired. After dropping his bag at his flat and changing clothes, he headed for a favorite pub on

Blackfriars Road. The room was abuzz with conversations. Glimpsing Anthony Miles at the bar, he sidled over to the stool next to him.

"How did your meeting with Dieter Wallach go?" Miles asked, sipping his pint of bitter.

"I'm trying my best to work with him. But it's very frustrating," Brighton sighed. "He's stubborn and incredibly process driven, and—well, just so *German*." He paused, seeing the slight twist at the corner of his colleague's mouth. "Yes, I know. I'm stereotyping."

"Indeed you are," his friend replied, "though one cannot deny there are differences in style between you and Dieter."

Brighton ordered a Guinness.

"Pardon me for saying this," Miles continued, "but you're not doing much for your own leadership prospects if you keep coming back to Callaghan with problems—especially if he starts to believe they spring from prejudices on your part. Think about it from his perspective. He's put together a deal that is perfectly sound from a strategic vantage point. He sees it as your job, and the rest of ours, to get behind it and make it work on the ground."

"But he has to acknowledge that this integration will be fundamentally different from the other ones we've managed!" Brighton blurted out. "It's hard enough to deal with different corporate cultures, but now we have all the additional complications of national differences." He lowered his voice. "And you know, it's not just Dieter. I keep hearing complaints from our people about how difficult it is dealing with the Germans. They don't think, act, work, or manage like we do. They take themselves far more seriously."

"Well, you're not going to budge Callaghan on that point. Remember what he said: 'Food people are food people.'" Miles added quietly: "I lived in Germany for a few years. Did you know that?"

"It doesn't show," Brighton said with a smirk. But he studied his friend's face. "OK. So go on."

"I had a girlfriend there," Miles recalled. "Ingrid. When I first met her, I kept thinking how serious she was. And organized!" He recalled that on their first date, she had welcomed him into an impeccably clean apartment. In the kitchen, the cups, plates, and glasses were displayed in a modern sideboard, with everything lined up just so.

"Sounds like a typical controlling German to me," Brighton observed.

"But she wasn't compulsive—Ingrid was actually quite adaptable." Miles paused. "And I began to appreciate the benefits of having that kind of structure around all the details of life. It can be quite comforting. I think you may be confusing that with being controlling.

"What's more," Miles continued, "once I got to know her better, I found she had this wonderful, irreverent sense of humor. In fact, she loved playing practical jokes on me. Maybe she thought I was the one who was too serious."

Brighton smiled. "I presume this is all by way of telling me that the problems I'm having with Dieter are really just a matter of perspective."

"Well, it's not for me to say," Miles noted. "But think about it. Ever since Callaghan took over, he has talked about how critical it is to have a global perspective. That's what he wants from his top managers. But what does it mean? Is it just thinking about what parts of the world we can sell more product in? Or is it more a question of seeing things in different ways?" Miles frowned for a moment. "Listen, you know more about these things than I do. But is that something you can train a manager to do? Stop thinking like a Brit or a German and start thinking at some higher level? Because if so, that's what your leadership development program should be aiming for."

Brighton took out his cash, ready to settle up. "Quite a speech," he said. He put the money on the bar and shrugged on his jacket. "But you're right, I'm sure. And it's absolutely true what you said earlier, that Callaghan is not going to tolerate any pesky cultural issues getting in the way of his grand plan. I appreciate the counsel."

Miles hadn't made a move to leave, though his glass was also drained. He appeared to be lost in thought.

Brighton ventured a guess: "So, that German girl. Sounds like you liked her very much. Whatever happened?"

Miles pushed his glass forward and sighed. "Yes, well. Perhaps we did prove too different in the end. Anyway, it didn't work out." He gave a little wave, letting Brighton know he could go on without him.

Can a Clash of Cultures Undermine this Cross-Border Merger?

Five commentators offer expert advice.

➤ Robert F. Bruner

Robert F. Bruner (brunerr@virginia.edu) serves as a Distinguished Professor and the executive director of the Batten Institute at the University of Virginia's Darden Graduate School of Business Administration in Charlottesville. His new book is Applied Mergers and Acquisitions *(Wiley, 2004).*

A culture clash can indeed undermine this merger. Witness Volvo and Renault's attempted 1993 merger, which was canceled in part because of doubts that the French and Swedes could get along. Sony's acquisition of Columbia Pictures in 1989 triggered a $3.2 billion write-off in 1994, largely because the Japanese didn't succeed in understanding or managing the cultural aberrations of Hollywood. And in 1998, Daimler and Chrysler imposed waves of culture shock on each other, some of which are still resounding.

Despite Thomas Jefferson's declaration that the spirit of commerce knows no country, those who practice commerce are deeply shaped by their cultural roots. It's difficult enough for two domestic firms with markedly different cultures to combine. But in a cross-border context, opportunities for equals to misunderstand and disagree multiply like weeds. Differences in language, customs, values, and training shout that the two firms in this story are not equals, a reality confirmed by Royal Biscuit's dominance of the management and supervisory boards.

Moreover, most so-called mergers of equals aren't equal at all. More often than not, the acquiring company cloaks the merger in a false amity designed to disguise painful organizational and economic realities from the target company's employees and shareholders. Ultimately, calling the deal a merger of equals simply worsens internal power struggles, because it defers the ultimate reckoning on who will rule.

Despite the difficulties inherent in a cross-border merger, there is a glimmer of hope for Royal Edeling, provided the CEO, John Callaghan, makes the vision for the new company clear and appealing to parties on both sides and gives his managers sufficient authority to implement it. One hallmark of a great merger is the creation of business approaches that neither company could have undertaken on its own. Callaghan should focus the executive teams and boards of both companies on developing a new vision, a clear set of expectations, a solid operating style, and a culture that draws upon and respects the Anglo and German traditions but rises above nationalism.

Callaghan needs the help of HR heads Michael Brighton and Dieter Wallach, but he can't force them onto the bandwagon simply by fiat. Temper tantrums, intimidation, and threats won't work to create a more unified culture; indeed, his fury has the effect of further dividing the middle managers and increasing their timidity. Brighton and Wallach are understandably confused, and they don't feel they have the authority to act on their own. Callaghan will do much better with them if he makes it clear that he understands their fears and if he challenges them to rise to the occasion. He should turn the tables by telling them he wants them to take a direct role in inventing the new way. He needs to express Royal Edeling's "cause" in compelling terms and enlist everyone in it.

For their part, Brighton and Wallach should realize that they have taken the path of least resistance; they have merely pooled good ideas from each side without asking how the whole can be greater than the sum of the parts. They need to start fresh with a creative plan that surprises and delights Callaghan. It will require leading from the middle. Though they may not have buy-in from their superiors, peers, or subordinates, they need to reach beyond the immediate task to align, inspire, and lend direction to those around them.

The first step toward leadership is personal rapport. Brighton would be wise to follow the advice and model of his friend Anthony Miles. He should invite Wallach out for a beer and try to develop a personal relationship with him. A shoptalk-free evening in which Michael discovers more about who Dieter really is as a human being might go a long way toward melting away stereotypes.

➤ Leda Cosmides and John Tooby

Leda Cosmides (cosmides@psych.ucsb.edu) and John Tooby (tooby@anth.ucsb.edu) are codirectors of the Center for Evolutionary Psychology at the University of California, Santa Barbara, and are editors of The Adapted Mind: Evolutionary Psychology and the Generation of Culture *(Oxford University Press, 1992).*

For Michael Brighton, there is a British "us" and a German "them." For Dieter Wallach, the "us" is German and the "them" is British. For both, "us" is trustworthy and competent, "them" is neither. Before the merger, Royal Biscuit and Edeling were what psychologists call rival coalitions in a zero-sum game. Each was a highly cooperative group whose members coordinated their behavior to achieve a common goal: taking market share from "them."

Is the difference in cultural norms causing the impasse? Or is Brighton's and Wallach's dislike of each other's norms a result of their previous membership in rival coalitions?

In the wake of World War II, psychologists, like everyone else, were wondering how the Holocaust could have happened. Is there something fundamentally different about German people or German culture? Or is there something universal in human nature—something triggered by particular kinds of situations—that causes people to see the world as a zero-sum game between rival coalitions?

In the 1950s, psychologist Muzafer Sherif randomly divided an ethnically homogenous sample of 11-year-old boys into two groups at a camp. During the first week, neither group knew about the other. The boys hiked together and engaged in cooperative work and games with other group members. The groups were then introduced to each other and told they would be competing in a tournament. Within a day, the boys were beginning to sound like Brighton and Wallach. Each group was derogating the skills, character, and norms of the other and bragging about its own. Within two days, small-scale warfare broke out between the groups, complete with fistfights, commando raids on cabins, and improvised weapons. (Counselors intervened to protect the boys.) The results of studies like this were crystal clear: The programs that create an us-versus-them psychology are present in everyone and easy to activate.

Why is this so? Natural selection equipped the human mind with a set of programs, each specialized for solving a problem faced by our hunter-gatherer ancestors. Our ancestors lived in bands; their lives depended on their ability to cooperate with group members and defend against rival groups. Neighboring bands were sometimes friendly but sometimes not. That which was most precious might be lost in a day—children killed, women taken as wives, foraging territories seized.

A fight is a conflict between two individuals, but a war is a conflict between two coalitions, each of which must coalesce and function as a cooperative unit. This poses specific problems, solved by specialized programs. To defend

---

Once the CEO focuses the merged company on a new goal, rival "them"s will become a united "us."

---

against a rival coalition or launch a raid, individuals must be able to do three things: coordinate their behavior with one another to achieve a common goal, share the resulting benefits with others who participated, and exclude free riders from these benefits. The common goal of competing against a rival coalition in a zero-sum game leads to cooperation among "us." Resources? Use them to strengthen "us," not "them." Attitudes? Build cooperation among your coalition mates and consider their strengths in forming a plan of action—and don't trust "them." Brighton and Wallach were coalitional rivals until recently; their attitudes are a product of their us-versus-them psychology, not the result of a culture clash.

In uniting two coalitions, a leader has to define the merged organization's common goals. Brighton, Wallach, and other executives will agree on methods once John Callaghan specifies which values the new leadership program should cultivate. And how can he get people to stop bickering? Instead of being content with Royal Edeling's position as the world's second-largest food company, he should focus his employees on a new goal: beating the competition and becoming number one. As this happens, the distrust and resentment within the newly blended Royal Edeling will gradually subside. Rival "them"s will become a united "us."

➤ Michael Pragnell

Michael Pragnell is the CEO and director of the board for the agribusiness firm Syngenta, headquartered in Basel, Switzerland.

The merger is in danger, not so much because of the nationalist differences but because John Callaghan has let the horse out of the barn too soon. Having delegated important tasks without giving Michael Brighton and Dieter Wallach a clear idea of the new company's overarching goals, he has abdicated his responsibility. Before he does anything else, Callaghan needs to call a halt to the troops. Then he must put together a balanced management team from both companies and lock that group in a room. He and the team must hammer out a completely fresh strategy, an organizational model, and guiding principles for the new company. Moreover, he should not compromise the new company's goals and values for the sake of making anyone comfortable. By failing to set a clear strategy and articulate a new value system before setting people loose on various projects, he has placed the merger in much worse jeopardy than it might otherwise be.

Still, Callaghan has my sympathies. His is not an easy position to be in. As the CEO of a company born from a giant international merger of equals, I've stood in his shoes. In 2000, my company, Syngenta, was formed from the marriage of the agribusinesses of two major pharmaceutical companies, the British firm AstraZeneca and the Swiss company Novartis. While our postmerger life has been successful, the planning process was not always smooth.

Strategically, the deal was designed as a merger of equals, the mutual goal of which was to build and sustain global leadership in the agribusiness industry. The executive board included eight members, four from each company. Reaching agreement on what we wanted to achieve was simple enough; the difficulty came in agreeing on implementation. We found ourselves embroiled in a number of contentious battles over organizational issues. One side wished to preserve its regional structure, under which powerful local managers oversaw control of everything from strategy to utilization of working assets. Their attitude was: Why try to fix something that isn't broken? The other company believed strongly that all of us in the new organization needed to break from our standard ways of doing things. I, for one, passionately believed that we needed to assume a new, broadly global stance with regard to product management, manufacturing operations, financial reporting, and research.

While we did not engage in nationalist antagonisms, our discussions were nonetheless sometimes extremely difficult. In the period between the announcement and the merger completion, we spent three months in closed sessions going over the same ground again and again. The experience was at times exhausting for all of us. In the end, however, logic and patience won the day. After we had hammered away at the same intractable issues, it became clear that if we were to succeed as a new company, we all would have to surrender our attachments to old ways of doing things. We would have to start afresh. We developed a completely new set of strategic criteria and corporate values to which neither company had previously ascribed, then communicated these to everyone at both companies.

Another huge challenge—one that certainly faces Royal Edeling—was the issue of overlap, or "cost synergies." At the outset, we had announced an estimated $525 million in cost savings. This meant that we had to make painful decisions regarding the more than 3,000 associated job cuts. To confront this issue, we assigned 100 task teams around the world to deliver the cost reductions. Within three months, the teams had solidified plans to do just that, and the teams hit the ground running the moment the new company was formed.

Finally, in almost each country, we moved everyone to new headquarters so that they would physically leave the past behind. Within a year, we were on solid footing, and our earlier culture clash was long forgotten.

➤ David Schweiger

David Schweiger (DMS@Schweiger-Assocates.com) is the president of the Columbia, South Carolina–based management consulting firm Schweiger and Associates and the author of M&A Integration: A Framework for Executives and Managers (McGraw-Hill, 2002).

The difficulty with the merger of Royal Biscuit and Edeling appears at first blush to be primarily cultural, but it's not. Although culture is often a source of conflict, there are other factors, such as personal stakes and interests, that are at work here. The disagreement between the two HR executives is primarily a managerial issue, and it needs to be addressed head-on, well before the final papers are signed.

At the end of the day, the issues that drive mergers such as this one into the ground are lack of honesty and objectivity and the failure of systematically applied transition management. The first thing John Callaghan needs to do is to stop pretending this is a merger of equals, because—as the German press already suspects—it isn't. It's clear that Royal Biscuit is the acquiring company. Refusal to acknowledge that will simply make employees and stockholders—

who are smarter than PR people think—at first skeptical and ultimately cynical. The political reality of the deal is that there is a winner and a loser. And the British company is the winner.

With this in mind, Callaghan should stop giving sound bites to the press and start delivering operational goals to his managers. He needs to clearly define and communicate the strategic and financial objectives underlying the merger. He must lay out the goals and the time frame for achieving them. Based on these, he also needs to create an integration transition structure and develop and implement a clear stakeholder communication plan.

Most important, he needs to shore up the staffing issues as quickly as possible. Despite assurances about jobs, people are worried about their survival. Clearly, this is on the minds of Michael Brighton and Dieter Wallach, who may be vying for the same job in the merged company. Neither they nor anyone else will begin to focus on work or truly cooperate until top management announces key positions from both companies. Regardless of the process, Callaghan must ensure that all employees are treated fairly, that key customers and employees stay on board, and that integration decisions are made objectively and implemented systematically.

Callaghan can't force Brighton and Wallach to get along, but he can challenge them by helping them recognize that they can either hang together or hang separately. He can do this by making the creation of a solid new leadership development plan part of their performance review. If they don't deliver, one or both of them may be out of a job. If they do, each will be assured of a place in the new organization. If it turns out that their jobs overlap, their successful collaboration might well lead to the creation of a new position for one or the other.

Given the prospect of an individual hanging, Brighton's and Wallach's minds will focus—and, it is to be hoped, move each from a position of defensiveness to one of learning, negotiation, and compromise. It would certainly behoove them to be as objective as possible. They should sit down and dispassionately articulate the desired outcomes of the project, including Callaghan's commitment to intercultural learning and a global mind-set. They can even map out on a piece of paper the pros and cons of various tactics for achieving leadership development goals. Similarities can lead them to common ground; dissimilarities can either lead to innovation or require compromises and trade-offs. If they find they are still not able to come to an agreement, they should seek the help of a facilitator. Theirs would certainly not be the first relationship that needed a marriage counselor. And if they fail, they will demonstrate that they are not the right people to manage leadership development for a CEO who is trying to create a firm with a global mind-set.

Originally published in May 2004

Reprint R0405A

ALDEN M. HAYASHI

Mommy-Track Backlash

Executive Summary

"Please don't tell me that I need to have a baby to have this time off." Those words were still ringing in the ears of Jessica Gonon an hour after a tense meeting with Jana Rowe, one of her key account managers.

Jessica, the vice president of sales and customer support at ClarityBase, considered Jana's request for a four-day workweek, for which she was willing to take a corresponding 20% cut in pay. Although the facts seemed simple, the situation was anything but. Just last week, Davis Bennett, another account manager, had made a similar request. He wanted a lighter workload so he could train for the Ironman Triathlon

Executive Summary

World Championship. Both Jana and Davis were well aware that Megan Flood, another account manager, had been working a reduced schedule for nearly two years. When she was hired, Megan had requested Fridays off to spend time with her two young sons. And since she came highly recommended and the talent pool was tight, Jessica had agreed to the arrangement.

The eight account managers at ClarityBase were in charge of helping the company's largest clients install and maintain database applications, which often required no small amount of hand-holding and coddling. Because Megan had an abbreviated schedule, the other account managers were assigned the more difficult clients. But if Jessica agreed to a shorter workweek for Jana and Davis, who would take on the toughest customers? And what would happen if the other account managers started asking for similar deals?

How can Jessica maintain the productivity of her department and meet her staff's needs for flexible work schedules while striking an equitable solution for both parents and nonparents? Four experts advise Jessica on her next move in this fictional case study.

Please don't tell me that I need to have a baby to have this time off."

Those words were still ringing in the ears of Jessica Gonon an hour after a tense meeting with one of her key managers. As she sat in her office trying to make sense of a recent customer survey, Jessica, the vice president of sales and customer support at ClarityBase, was having trouble concentrating on the bar graphs and pie charts in front of her. Snippets from her earlier conversation kept interrupting her thoughts.

The issue seemed simple enough. Jana Rowe, an account manager in the sales support department, had requested a lighter workload: she wanted a four-day workweek, and for that she was willing to take a corresponding 20% cut in pay. Those were the simple facts, but the situation at ClarityBase was anything but straightforward.

Just last week, Davis Bennett, another account manager, had made a similar request. He wanted a lighter workload so he could train for the Ironman Triathlon World Championship, the premier competition held each October in Hawaii. He was a world-class athlete, and his ultimate goal was a spot on the U.S. Olympic team in 2004. Davis had said he didn't need to begin training full throttle until mid-spring, so Jessica had asked him for a couple weeks to figure out how Clarity-Base might best accommodate his training schedule.

A complicating factor was that both Davis and Jana were well aware that Megan Flood, another account manager, had been working a reduced schedule for nearly two years. When she was hired, Megan had requested Fridays off to spend time with her two young boys, and Jessica had agreed.

In her meeting with Jessica, Jana had declined to explain why she wanted the reduced hours, citing "personal reasons." When Jessica had paused, wondering what those reasons might be, Jana added, "All I'm asking for is the same deal that Megan has. Please don't tell me that I need to have a baby to have this time off." Jana was married and had no children. Davis was single and also without children.

There were other subtle issues. A reduced workweek for Jana and Davis meant much more than just that. From Jessica's conversations with them, she inferred that any official reduction in hours—having a day off every week in Jana's case—would also mean they wouldn't have to work the occasional nights and weekends that the other account managers did, all except Megan.

ClarityBase, headquartered in Reston, Virginia, sold large database applications that helped companies run their operations, including human resources, manufacturing, and order fulfillment. The eight account managers—Jana, Davis, and Megan among them—were in charge of helping the company's largest customers install and maintain the software, which required no small amount of hand-holding and coddling. Because Megan had an abbreviated workweek, the other account managers were assigned the more demanding clients.

Davis, in particular, seemed to have the toughest customers, most notably St. Elizabeth's Hospital in Philadelphia, which required him to be available around-the-clock. Once, when its system failed on Christmas Day, Davis took the train to Philadelphia to help get the hospital's crucial patient database up and running. If Jessica agreed to a shorter workweek for Jana and Davis, who would take over clients like St. Elizabeth's? And what would happen if the other account managers began asking for similar deals?

It was Monday morning—what a way to start the week, thought Jessica. She had promised Jana that she'd get back to her by Friday, so at least she had the whole week to sort things out. That was plenty of time, or so she hoped.

Trading Places

Jessica had had second thoughts before hiring Megan—she had made so many demands in the interview. Her children, said Megan, were paramount to her, and she wanted a very flexible schedule. Not only did she want the freedom to come in late and leave early occasionally, she also wanted Fridays off. She wasn't amenable to any business travel, and she wouldn't be able to attend after-hours meetings except when her personal schedule allowed.

But Megan had come highly recommended. Her three years of experience at Dawson Software, Clarity-Base's chief competitor, would be a huge asset; her technical skills were superb; and her professional and friendly demeanor would surely impress customers. And, last but certainly not least, Jessica had looked for months to hire someone of Megan's caliber. None of the other candidates had come remotely close. So after thinking about it over a weekend, Jessica decided to offer her the job.

Still, Megan's demands had left Jessica feeling uneasy. Part of the reason, Jessica realized later after much introspection, was because she had had it much tougher when she was starting her career in the early 1970s—a different era before flexible work hours, on-site day care centers, and the Family and Medical Leave Act. At that time, women like Jessica, who held a bachelor's degree in computer programming from Penn State, simply couldn't have it all, both career and children. So Jessica and her husband, who was on the partner track at his architectural firm, had decided that she would quit her job as a supervisor in the MIS department for Capital Insurance when they had their first child.

Nine years later, after their youngest child had started kindergarten, Jessica reentered the workforce as a sales assistant at ClarityBase. She took classes at night to get up to speed on the computer industry and slowly rose to become a sales rep, then account manager, and then head of the Northeast sales region. At the age of 52, she was promoted to her current position of vice president of sales and customer support. The road had been long, and having children had been a substantial detour. But just because Jessica had had to make trade-offs between career and family, should Megan have to as well?

Hidden Tensions

It was nearly 7 PM when Jessica finally crammed the customer survey reports into her briefcase and started to head home. As she walked through the sales-support group, she was reminded of a conversation she happened to overhear in this corridor last week: "I honestly don't know if I can force myself to smile through yet another precious baby shower," said a woman's voice from the other side of a cubicle wall. At the time, Jessica paid little attention to the comment, but now, those words made her stop and think.

ClarityBase prided itself on its progressive work-life policies. The company offered all employees family medical insurance, adoption assistance, and paid maternity and paternity leave. But perhaps the thing that ClarityBase was most proud of was the on-site child care center that the company subsidized. Bill Welensky, vice president of human resources, liked to brag that such perks helped ClarityBase keep employee turnover to less than 5% annually, unheard of in the software industry. But had the company become too pro-parent at the expense of other employees?

> **ClarityBase prided itself on its progressive work-life policies. But had the company become too pro-parent at the expense of other employees?**

A year and a half ago, as Labor Day approached, tension between the two groups surfaced. Ed Fernandez—whom Jessica had just hired to supervise ClarityBase's call center—had drawn up the schedule for the holiday weekend in what he thought was the fairest way: people who hadn't worked over a holiday for the longest time would be the first to be called to duty. Many mothers were on the short list because the previous supervisor had never scheduled them to work on holidays. When the assignments were posted, the mothers were peeved, and their reaction irritated other employees.

Fortunately, Ed was able to strike a compromise. The assignments for Labor Day would be done as they had been in the past, with special consideration given to mothers. From that point on, though, every employee would have to work his or her fair share of holidays, regardless of past status or history. The only consideration would be for seniority: newer employees, whether they were parents or not, would be the first to serve.

That solution seemed to prevent a fracture in the workplace between parents and nonparents. But could it be that a dangerous rift did exist, with only a fragile veneer of social decorum to conceal it? Jessica did an about-face and headed back to her office to reboot her computer. She composed two e-mails, one to Jana and the other to Davis, requesting that she meet with each of them as soon as possible to discuss their requests further.

Gathering Information

At lunch the next day, Jessica waited until she and Jana had comfortably settled into their booth and ordered their meals before asking the delicate question. "I want to understand your situation, why you've requested a shorter workweek," she started. "Yesterday, you cited 'personal reasons.' The last thing I want to do is pry into your personal life, but is there anything else you would feel comfortable telling me?"

Jessica watched as Jana swallowed her food and collected her thoughts. "I don't mean to be disrespectful,"

Jana began. "Honestly, I don't. Nor do I mean to be mysterious. But I really don't think I should have to explain why I want the time off. Suffice it to say that it's very, very important to me."

"I see," replied Jessica. "I'm sorry to have asked. I just wanted to understand your situation better."

The two women ate in silence for a few minutes. Then Jana put her fork down and looked at Jessica intently. "The thing that gets me," Jana said, "is that somehow all the family stuff is deemed more important—the soccer games, the school plays, the graduations. Well, I have important things going on in my life, too. They just don't involve children."

"Do you think that parents are treated with favoritism at ClarityBase?" Jessica asked.

"I'd like to think not," Jana replied. "But is it so hard to believe that my reasons for wanting a lighter workload might be just as important to me as Megan's children are to her?" Before Jessica could say anything, Jana added, "Don't get me wrong. I think Megan's great. She's one of our best account managers, so I have no qualms about the deal she has. I'm just saying that I think I deserve the same deal."

On her drive home that night, Jessica thought more about what Jana had said. She had heard of companies with a no-explanation policy for time off, but that blanket policy seemed unfair to her. Some people might need more consideration at a specific time—for example, the birth of a child—whereas others could postpone their plans—for instance, a college course could be taken in the fall instead of in the spring. On the other hand, a blanket no-explanation policy would certainly make her job easier—she wouldn't have to make value judgments about whose reasons were more important.

Breakfast the next morning with Davis went more smoothly. When Jessica asked him whether he felt that parents at ClarityBase were treated with favoritism, he replied, "I've never felt like a second-class citizen, if that's what you're asking. I really don't mind helping out someone who's having some kind of family emergency, because working parents have it tough. I have no idea how they juggle everything. I'd be a nut case."

"Thanks for your great attitude," said Jessica.

"Well, we're all on the same team."

"I guess what I need to know from you," Jessica continued, "is how much flexibility you might have. Excuse my ignorance, but I know very little about triathletes, and I'm not sure how much time off you'll need to train."

"It varies; everyone seems to have a different training regimen," said Davis. "But here's what I think would work best for me: for the summer, I'd like to leave work at 3 on Tuesdays and Thursdays. Then, during the fall, I'd want to leave early maybe four days a week. But on the days I left early, I could definitely come in at 6 AM to make up some of that time, or I could stay later on the other days."

"I appreciate that," said Jessica, "and I've always been grateful for your willingness to go the extra mile. But with this new schedule, do you think you could keep up with the needs of your clients?"

"I've thought about that a lot and, to be honest with you, I don't know," Davis admitted. "I realize that the customer comes first, but I'd also like to think that most of them would be willing to make adjustments—and I think they'd be minor ones—to accommodate my new hours. Of course, I have no idea if everything would work out as smoothly as I'm hoping."

"This particular triathlon is really important to you?" Jessica asked, almost rhetorically.

"Well, I've won a few local ones, but nothing big," said Davis. "And the Ironman is big; it's the Superbowl. My goal is to place in the top 20. And, yes, it's very important to me. In fact, I suppose I've never wanted anything as badly in my entire life."

Jessica thought back to when she had hired Davis more than five years ago. What impressed her most about him was his passion. Davis was clearly the type of person who threw himself into everything he did, and it was evident in his work. So it was hardly surprising that he would want extra training time to prepare for the Ironman.

Decision Time

As Jessica pulled into ClarityBase's parking lot, she noticed a Honda with a bumper sticker that proudly declared "Child-*free* (not child-*less*) . . . and loving every minute of it." Could that car belong to the woman she had overheard the other night.

Before heading to her office, Jessica decided to stop by the HR department to talk with Bill Welensky. "Bill, do you have a few free minutes?" she asked.

Bill, who was Jessica's mentor and one of her biggest supporters at ClarityBase, listened carefully as she told him about Jana, Davis, and her earlier arrangement with Megan. "I know that we don't have any official policy that specifically addresses these issues," she said, "but I was hoping for some advice."

"I'm not sure exactly what to say," said Bill. "As you know, ClarityBase prides itself on its progressive views on work-life issues, and we try to accommodate people as much as possible. But we really don't have any policies at all regarding flex time."

When Jessica told Bill about what Jana had said— that she felt parents got special consideration at ClarityBase—he paused before speaking. "That's not the first time that sentiment has been expressed," he offered. "But as far as flex time or shorter workweeks are concerned, we certainly don't have any guidelines with regard to parents versus nonparents. Supervisors just have to make those kinds of decisions on a case by case basis."

Jessica thought about that for a few seconds. "The problem," she started, "is that I feel like I somehow have to make value judgments about what's more important, someone's parenting needs versus someone else's personal achievement goals. And I don't feel comfortable doing that."

Bill looked at Jessica. "Have you tried taking a different perspective?" he asked. "Think of it as two employees who both want raises but your budget will allow just one. What would you do?"

Without hesitation, Jessica replied, "I'd make a judgment about just how valuable—and irreplaceable—each employee was. But my situation is so much more complicated than that. With salary requests, I could compare apples with apples. With work-life issues, I feel like I have to compare an apple with a hammer with a vase."

"Then let me speak to you as a friend and not as the HR director," Bill said. "And let me be frank with you: the reason you were promoted to vice president is precisely because of your ability to compare apples with hammers and vases. You run a large department and, yes, it's not always easy to meet the needs of your staff while also making your quarterly numbers. So, no, you can't go out and hire two more account managers to cover for the people who want flex time. There is no simple, tidy solution here."

As Jessica left Bill's office, she tried to reassure herself that it was just Wednesday; she still had until Friday to figure out what to do. The problem, though, was that with each day she was becoming increasingly confused.

How Should Jessica Stem the Backlash?

Four commentators offer their advice.

➤ # Michele S. Darling

Michele S. Darling is the executive vice president of corporate governance and human resources at Prudential Insurance Company of America in Newark, New Jersey.

Jessica Gonon needs an entirely new mind-set. She has been shouldering too much on her own. But she doesn't need to figure out how to make flexible schedules work, her staff does. If they want flexible schedules, they need to devise ways to make them work within the context of achieving the department's business goals and objectives.

When Davis Bennett, for example, made his request, Jessica asked him very reasonable questions, such as whether he could continue to meet the needs of his clients. But his response was that he wasn't sure, as if it were now her problem to solve. It's not. If Davis and Jana Rowe want to change their schedules, they need to figure out how to make that work.

From my experience, I believe that no corporate policies, programs, or guidelines can cover all of the myriad work-life situations that are bound to arise. And I have found that, nine times out of ten, people will come up with more creative and better solutions for meeting their needs for flexible work hours than their managers or someone sitting in my chair could have.

That said, Jessica should provide the tools her people will need to make their strongest cases for flexible time. She should start by sitting down with Bill Welensky of HR to devise guidelines for employee proposals for flexible work arrangements. The format should specify what each proposal must contain: what work needs to be managed during this period of time, how the person will do that work so that the schedule is seamless to customers, what hours the person is proposing to work, and so on.

She should give Jana and Davis the guidelines and encourage them to think of creative ways of achieving flexibility while also getting their jobs done. She should suggest that they consider as many options as possible, such as telecommuting and job sharing with another account manager.

Since Jessica has realized that a rift between parents and nonparents might be developing in her department, she should call a departmental meeting to tell people that she is open to flexible work hours for everyone, regardless of their reasons for wanting them. But, she should add, it's up to each individual to make a strong business case for the change. "As far as I'm concerned," Jessica might say, "the reason for your request is irrelevant. I don't care if you want to leave early on Wednesdays to take your son to baseball practice or to take a class. You just need to explain how you're going to continue to get your work done."

When Jessica declines a request, she needs to give specific reasons for her decision. Perhaps the applicant hasn't sufficiently demonstrated how he will meet his customers' needs. Or maybe the employee fails to explain the details of her job-sharing arrangement. Jessica should then give the person a chance to revise the proposal for her reconsideration.

Jessica might also encourage her eight account managers to think as a team. Collectively, they might devise a new way to get their work done while also ensuring that their personal needs are being met. Again, Jessica might offer suggestions, such as having two or more account managers for demanding customers like St. Elizabeth's Hospital.

Of course, for many situations, flexible arrangements are inherently difficult, such as with call-center operations. Even then, however, people often come up with effective solutions. At Prudential Insurance, we have found that telecommuting can work even for employees in a call center. With the right technology, it doesn't matter where the employee is physically located.

Jessica's task won't be easy. But by encouraging her staff to come up with creative solutions, she can go a long way toward meeting their needs.

➤ Chris Dineen

Chris Dineen is the director of finance at RadView Software in Burlington, Massachusetts.

Jessica's confusion is understandable. Like many companies, ClarityBase has tried to create a family-friendly environment, but it hasn't developed any overall guidelines or policies to do so. Jessica needs to examine her situation from the inside out, starting with the trees before tending to the forest.

At its core, the problem is simple—Jessica must maintain the performance of her department while ensuring that the members of her staff are content with the balance they have struck between their professional and personal lives. Obviously, Jessica must first determine just how many of her account managers can be on a reduced workload.

Let's assume that Jessica's department can afford to have only one additional person on a reduced workload, so she needs to decide between Jana and Davis. Jessica attempted to learn why each of them desired a reduced schedule to help her base her decision on whose situation had greater merit. While Davis was forthcoming in explaining the reason for his request, Jana chose to keep her details confidential. Understandably, Jessica doesn't want to pry into Jana's personal life, but this information could be crucial. Consider an extreme example: what if Jana wanted Wednesdays free so that she could do some freelance work for a competitor of ClarityBase?

Bill, the head of HR, suggested that Jessica view her dilemma from a different perspective by thinking of two employees who both want a raise that only one of them can have. If Jana asked Jessica for a salary increase without being able to justify her request, Jessica would have little difficulty saying no. In other words, both Jana and Davis need to make their strongest cases for their requests for reduced hours, and Jessica must then decide between them. If Jana, for whatever reason, fails to present a compelling case, then Jessica has no other choice but to make a decision based on the limited information she has.

But there might be a larger issue here. Megan, the working mother, is generally precluded from working evenings and weekends because of family obligations. Perhaps Jana's request is really a protest against having to bear the burden of longer hours and tougher clients. Jana may see a reduced workload as the only way to resolve what she perceives as unfair work allocation.

That said, Jessica should explore alternatives to achieve an equitable solution among *all* of the account managers, both parents and nonparents. Not that she should renege on her deal with Megan—after all, Megan joined Clarity-Base with the understanding that the company would accommodate her parenting needs. But maybe Jessica could implement a policy in which account managers accumulate overtime hours that they can use later for time off. Or she might consider giving additional compensation, such as bonuses and raises, to employees bearing a heavier burden of the workload—if she isn't already doing so.

Jessica also has to consider the broad impact of her decisions. If Megan, Jessica, and Davis worked reduced hours, would others on her staff insist on the same thing? More generally, would employees in other departments also seek to receive similarly reduced workloads?

Thinking about those questions, Jessica can now begin to look at the forest. She'll need to let Bill know what she's doing because her actions may very well set a de facto policy for the rest of ClarityBase. Perhaps it is now Jessica's turn to give Bill some advice: he should quickly call a meeting of the senior executives at ClarityBase to discuss the company's need to establish official policies and guidelines on work-life and family issues. Otherwise, managers like Jessica will be creating those policies in an ad hoc fashion.

➤ Elinor Burkett

Elinor Burkett is the author of The Baby Boon: How Family-Friendly America Cheats the Childless *(Free Press, 2000). She is a journalist, and her articles have appeared in the* Miami Herald, New York Times Magazine, *the* Atlantic Monthly, Rolling Stone, *and* Mirabella.

Jessica is confronted with one of the stickiest issues in HR today: how to clean up the mess created by an ill-considered rush into family-friendly workplaces. When businesses like ClarityBase began offering special considerations to working parents, they failed to consider that granting one group of employees such privileges adds up, perforce, to inferior treatment for the rest of the workforce.

Of course, employers have long engaged in inequitable practices, but they have traditionally done so to encourage and reward merit or tenure—*not* worker fertility. If you consider the dollar value of ClarityBase's benefits packages as a form of compensation, you'll quickly see that the company has changed those rules. As a result, employees like Jana and Davis know that no matter how hard, long, or well they work, they can't achieve remunerative parity with their peers who are parents. Even if they were to receive huge merit bonuses and salary raises, their total compensation would still fall short of what they would have been receiving had they been parents doing the same work.

That's no way to maintain employee morale. Ask any manager of a Marxist enterprise who tried to run a business guided by the principle "from each according to his ability, to each according to his need." The result has typically been employee apathy, which leads to lackluster performance. After all, why go the extra mile when it won't be rewarded?

In trying to resolve the dilemma created by her company's departure from a merit-based compensation system, Jessica was right to cringe from standing in judgment on the relative value of what her employees proposed to do with their requested time off. Doing so is not only a dangerous invasion of employee privacy; it is demeaning, particularly in a diverse society. Should a gay employee with a sick partner be forced to come out to get leave to care for him? Should a Mormon staffer have to explain the importance of working one day a week as a missionary?

Executives who manage their workforces in that fashion set themselves up as the applause meter in the old TV game show *Queen for a Day*, with staff members forced to compete for the title of "employee most needy of consideration." But workplace benefits should not be contest prizes; they should be rewards for jobs well done.

And that is precisely the solution to Jessica's conundrum: she needs to recognize that benefits and flexibility are as integral to employee compensation packages as are paychecks, and she must uniformly apply the time-proven standard of equal pay for equal work when handing out assignments and perks. "Pay is for work done, rather than for the number of dependents of the workers," asserted Secretary of Labor Lewis Baxter Schwellenbach in the 1940s, when he argued for the Equal Pay Act. A company that adheres to that standard does not adjust the salaries of people according to their number of dependents, nor does it limit health insurance benefits only to workers with kids. Similarly, businesses must treat time and other nonfinancial benefits with the same dependent-neutral hand.

So Jessica needn't think about the relative merits of what her employees do with their free time; that is not her legitimate concern. Instead, she should judge the relative value of those employees in the workplace context, which is most certainly her business, and reward them accordingly. And if she is hesitant to use merit as her criterion, she has only two alternatives: either she must hire enough staff to allow everyone flex time, or she must give all employees equal access to it by devising some sort of rotation schedule, which would necessitate limiting any single employee's right to flex time to, say, a year.

The main point is parity—an acknowledgment that childless employees have as much right to their personal lives as working parents do. And if Jessica doesn't strive toward such equality at ClarityBase, then she had better be prepared to spend months searching for replacements for both Davis and Jana, replacements who are willing to be treated as second-class employees.

➢ Stewart D. Friedman

Stewart D. Friedman is the director of Ford's Leadership Development Center in Dearborn, Michigan. He is on leave from the University of Pennsylvania's Wharton School of Business, where he directs the Work/Life Integration Project. He recently published, with Jeff Greenhaus, Work and Family—Allies or Enemies? *(Oxford, 2000).*

The goal is equity, not equality. Everyone's life outside of work should be treated with respect, but not necessarily identically. Jessica needs to embrace her employees' diversity by supporting their different passions. If she makes an effort to meet the personal-life needs of each individual on her staff, she will increase the vitality and commitment of her department.

The key is flexibility, which has to run both ways, from organization to employee and vice versa. To encourage this two-way flow, Jessica should let her staff know what the dilemmas are and work with them to find solutions. Jessica should meet with each of the eight account managers individually and say, "I want to create an environment where we all respect and support one another, in terms of both our business and personal goals. I'd like for us all to talk about our expectations—in all areas of our lives—as a group. Then we can begin to figure out collectively how to meet those expectations in creative ways that benefit all facets of each person: work, home, community, and self."

Jessica must encourage both Jana and Megan to participate in the discussion, touchy as this might be. Jessica might explain to them that if all team members share their personal priorities, then the opportunities for easy fixes or for leveraging complementary or synergistic interests increase, for the benefit of all. "For example," Jessica might say, "if you were writing a novel in your spare time and Davis were having trouble with his customer Blackhill and Hansen Publishing, you might switch clients with him so that you could develop editorial contacts at B&H." The subtext here, and the main message to her team, is, "We're all in this together."

To arrive at win-win solutions, Jessica and her team must recognize and discuss the demands of the business as well as life outside ClarityBase. This is the essence of what I call "total leadership," which integrates work, home, community, and self. Because ClarityBase has only valued the personal life goals linked to parenthood, there's a legitimate sense of resentment among those without kids at the company. All the more reason for each individual to express what's most important to him or her and for Jessica to encourage employees to recognize, respect, and support those priorities.

This discussion is the tricky part, but it's also where the real breakthroughs occur. People must be encouraged to assume that there are opportunities for achieving their goals in different ways—inside and outside of work—so they don't take a rigid position of, say, "I have to have Thursday mornings off." If employees state their expectations without asserting fixed positions or demands, the dialogue will take off from there.

In looking for creative solutions, Jessica and her team should consider different ways to satisfy customers, especially through the use of technology. Some clients might accept—even welcome—more e-mail and voice mail communications to cut down on the need for face-to-face meetings.

And to ensure that individuals are treated equitably, the team must consider whether certain account managers should receive higher compensation for handling more demanding clients. Perhaps each customer should have a degree-of-difficulty rating. With such a system, some account managers might even prefer difficult clients because of the higher compensation.

That's where Ed, the call-center supervisor, went wrong in scheduling his staff for Labor Day. He made assumptions about what people wanted without establishing a dialogue about what was most important to them. For all he knew, some people might have preferred working on holidays, especially if they would be paid extra for it.

Bill in HR uses the word "accommodate," implying a traditional, zero-sum approach to the connection between work and personal life. Jessica should instead look for synergies across the different domains of her staff's lives. By doing so, she might better tap into their passions and gain the benefits of total leadership: better business results and enriched lives.

Originally published in March 2001
Reprint R0103A

JOHN HUMPHREYS

The Best of Intentions

Executive Summary

Cynthia Mitchell has finally gotten a plum management opportunity at AgFunds, a Houston-based company that provides financial services to farmers and farmer-owned cooperatives. Peter Jones, regional vice president, has recruited Cynthia to revive the Arkansas district, which has been losing customers for 15 years. The sales force there isn't bad; it's just been poorly managed by an indifferent boss for too long. Still, Cynthia knows she'll need at least one powerhouse sales rep to get things back on track.

She thinks she's found that person in Steve Ripley, this year's top trainee at AgFunds, who is inexplicably available three months after the training period is over. In the interview, he proves to be ambitious, intelligent, and personable. But several of Cynthia's colleagues suggest that Steve might not be the best fit for the job: He's a black man in a company whose customer base is mostly conservative and white. Uncomfortably recalling her own experiences at Ag-Funds—she'd been rejected for a position in a territory that was deemed too unfriendly to female sales reps—Cynthia addresses the issue with Peter.

The mostly white farmers in Cynthia's district just won't trust their books to a black professional, Peter explains. And other minority professionals at Ag-Funds have derailed their careers trying to make inroads in unfriendly districts. "Steve deserves to start out in a more hospitable district. Once the right opportunity opens up, he'll be hired, and he'll do brilliantly," Peter reassures Cynthia, but she's still uncertain. Should she ignore her customers' biases and hire Steve, possibly setting him up to fail? Or would it be better to let Steve wait for a friendlier opportunity? Four experts comment on this fictional case study.

Cynthia Mitchell just stared at her boss, Peter Jones. She admired him a great deal, but she couldn't believe what she had just heard.

"Let me get this straight," she said. "I shouldn't give Steve Ripley this assignment, even though he's the most qualified candidate, because the clients won't let him succeed?"

"It's your decision—and Steve's, if you decide to offer him the job. But I think it would be a big mistake," Peter replied.

"Because he's black," Cynthia prompted. "And because we're automatically assuming that the mostly white farmers in this district won't trust their books to a black professional?"

Peter flushed. "We don't assume it. We know it. Just ask Betty Inez and Hugh Conley. They were every bit as good as Ripley. But we—okay, I was blind to the unpleasant reality that plenty of discrimination still exists out there, like it or not. Because of my ignorance, they both failed miserably in districts that looked a lot like this one. It wasn't their fault, but their careers with AgFunds got derailed anyway. I want to give Steve a fighting chance, and I want AgFunds to have a better record developing minority managers."

Cynthia sighed. "This feels all wrong to me, Peter, but I know you wouldn't raise the issue if it didn't have any substance. Let me think about it."

Personal Experience

And think about it she did. Cynthia had flown to Houston earlier in the week for AgFunds' regional district managers meeting and had been enjoying getting to know her colleagues over dinners at a variety of excellent restaurants—a welcome relief from her rural Arkansas district, where the culinary choices ran the gamut from barbecue to, well, barbecue. She was new at her job, and the other district managers—all white men—had made her feel welcome and offered her survival tips.

Tonight, though, she stayed put at her hotel. First she worked out in the gym, then she ordered a Caesar salad and a beer from room service. While she waited for the food, she took a quick shower. When she finally settled down to her meal, she found she didn't have any appetite. The situation with Steve Ripley was making her really tense. It brought up bad memories. She sat back, sipped her beer, and remembered how her own career at AgFunds had started.

It wasn't so long ago. A Minnesota native with an undergraduate degree from Purdue, Cynthia had earned an MBA from the University of Kansas. She wanted to stay in the Midwest, and she wanted to work with the agricultural community. She had originally planned to pursue a career with the Chicago

---

"Let me get this straight," she said. "I shouldn't give Steve Ripley this assignment, even though he's the most qualified candidate, because the clients won't let him succeed?"

Board of Trade, but the opportunities there hadn't seemed promising. AgFunds—a financial services company specializing in investments and accounting services for farmers and farmer-owned cooperatives—had pursued her aggressively. She had joined the firm as an investment trainee in the Chicago office after graduation, just four years ago. Her first year wasn't that different from being in school; she spent most of her time studying for the exams she had to take to become a fully licensed representative. She thrived in the competitive training environment and was considered the top graduate in her class.

The best trainees that year were all vying for a position in northern Indiana. Mike Graves, a highly successful investment rep, was being promoted to district manager. Within six years, Mike had turned a declining stream of clients in Indiana into one of the company's largest and most coveted portfolios. Cynthia wanted the job badly and was sure she had a good shot at it. Her interview with Mike went well, or so she thought. She was half planning the move to Indiana when she received an e-mail announcing that the job had gone to her fellow trainee Bill Hawkins. She was genuinely surprised. Bill was a great guy, but his credentials didn't measure up to hers. In fact, she'd spent a lot of time tutoring him after he failed an early licensing test.

When she ran into Mike shortly thereafter, she congratulated him on his promotion. He seemed self-conscious, and before long he stumbled into an explanation for why she hadn't been picked for the plum job: "Eventually you'll be a better rep than Bill. I know it, and you know it. But this just wasn't the right territory for you. It's very conservative. Our customers wouldn't be comfortable doing business with a woman. One day you'll thank me for not putting you into a situation where you'd fail."

Thank him? Cynthia had felt more like strangling him. But, like a good sport, she offered him some politically correct conciliatory statements—"I'm sure you made the right choice; you know the territory," and so forth—and kept looking. A month later, she landed a less appealing but perfectly adequate sales rep's position in a northern Ohio district. Presumably, the district was more hospitable to women, though she'd had to prove herself to plenty of crusty male customers. Cynthia had done extremely well in the three years she spent there—well enough to be considered a rising star at AgFunds. So she wasn't surprised when Peter, the Houston-based regional vice president who oversaw eight southern districts in Arkansas, Louisiana, Mississippi, New Mexico, and Texas, recruited her to run the Arkansas district. The new position was a stretch; reps didn't usually get promoted this quickly, but she felt ready for the challenge.

And it definitely was a challenge. Arkansas was once a great district, but it had been losing customers for 15 years, thanks to a 25-year veteran who had gotten more and more comfortable in coasting mode. Peter had finally pushed the guy into early retirement and brought Cynthia in to shake things up. The sales force wasn't that bad; it had just been poorly managed. But Cynthia desperately needed at least one powerhouse rep. Privately, she admitted to herself that what she really needed was a clone of herself four years ago—somebody fresh out of school who was talented, ambitious, and extremely hungry.

She considered recruiting the second-best rep from her old region (he happened to be a good friend), but she wanted to look first at the recent crop of eager trainees. She was intrigued to discover that Steve Ripley, this year's top trainee, was inexplicably available three months after the training period had ended. He looked great on paper: a recent MBA from UCLA, a successful summer internship at AgFunds, a stint overseas as an economic analyst for the U.S. government. So why he was still available? Poor interpersonal skills, perhaps? When she met Steve, Cynthia discovered that this was far from true. He was personable, quick-witted, bright, an excellent conversationalist. He was also a black man in a company whose workforce was overwhelmingly white.

She had interviewed Steve just this week, while she was in Houston for the off-site, and she had ended the meeting wondering, very simply, how she'd gotten so lucky and when he could start. Within a few hours, though, her curiosity about why he was still available had resurfaced. When she asked a few discreet questions, her fellow district managers in Arkansas were evasive; they seemed uncomfortable. The longest-tenured of them finally told her that Steve wasn't necessarily a great fit in some parts of their region and suggested that she discuss the situation with Peter before she made an offer.

Set Up to Fail?

Cynthia shifted uncomfortably in her hotel room chair. She poked at her salad with distaste then scraped at the label on her half-empty Saint Arnold beer as she replayed this morning's meeting with Peter in her mind.

It hadn't gone well.

"We need to talk about Steve Ripley," she had started. "He's a remarkable candidate. Why wouldn't I hire him if I could get him?"

"Your predecessor didn't think he was a good fit," Peter had said gently. "I have to tell you I think he was right. And it's not because I'm a bigot. I can see you're wondering about that. Steve's fantastic. He's one of the best trainees we've had through here in years. But the biggest customers in your district don't want to work with a black guy. It's as simple as that."

"So if some big customers are discriminatory, we'll let them dictate our hiring policy?" Cynthia had challenged.

Peter had winced at her remark. "Look, Steve's going to be outstanding. He just deserves to start out in a more hospitable district. Once the right opportunity opens up, he'll be hired, and he'll do brilliantly."

Cynthia, remembering the job she'd lost out on in Indiana, then countered by saying, "So Steve has far fewer opportunities open to him than other, less-qualified applicants do."

"I know it doesn't sound fair, and in one sense it isn't," Peter had said. "But if Steve fails in his first assignment, it becomes extremely difficult to promote him—we'll be accused of favoritism or the very worst form of affirmative action. And let's not forget we have some obligation to maximize profits. I can almost guarantee you that won't happen in your district if you hire Steve. If our customers won't buy from Steve, it hurts the shareholders, it hurts Steve, it hurts you. Okay? How is that a good thing?"

Cards on the Table

Cynthia didn't sleep well that night. She tossed around, half awake, half asleep, agonizing about what her next step should be. Could she hire Steve against the explicit advice of her new boss? What would it mean for her career if Peter turned out to be right, and Steve didn't work out? Undoubtedly the easiest course would be to keep looking, perhaps to hire her colleague from Ohio, who was, after all, a proven quantity. But that didn't feel right.

During one of those 3 AM moments of apparent clarity that so often come to insomniacs, Cynthia decided to lay things on the line with Steve. At 8 AM, she called his house and asked if they could meet for lunch. He agreed.

"Look, what I'm about to tell you is sensitive," she said four hours later as she faced Steve over glasses of bubbly water at the Daily Review Café. "So I'm taking a chance. But I'm sure you sense a lot of what I'm going to say, so let's just talk about it openly."

"Sure, what's up?" He looked both quizzical and slightly disappointed.

"Oh Lord, he expected an offer," she thought to herself. Cynthia took a deep breath and started by telling him the story of how she lost the job in northern Indiana to a less qualified candidate and how much that had bothered her. She filled him in on the conversation with Peter the day before. By the time she'd finished, he was leaning back in his chair, sipping his water, eyes narrowed.

"I'm not sure what to say," he offered after a pause.

"No need to say anything yet. The thing is," she continued, "this is a company where women and minorities can get ahead. I know that from personal experience. And I walked in knowing I had to work harder and perform better than other candidates. I'm sure you did, too. But the folks in senior positions sometimes decide what's best for candidates without consulting them. I know I resented that a lot when it happened to me. I don't want to continue that pattern. I'm not ready to offer you the job, but I do want you to know what's being talked about, and I'm curious to know what your response is."

Cynthia half expected Steve to start selling himself again, as he had during their initial interview—to ask for the chance to prove himself, even if it was a tough territory. But his response was more tempered than that.

"As long as we're being open with each other, I have to say I'm not sure. I'd like to stay in this part of the country for a few years, for personal reasons, but I don't want to take a job that sets me up for failure. There are other districts in this region where blacks have done well."

Cynthia was feeling deflated. "So—so you want to withdraw from being considered?"

"I didn't say that. I guess I want to be sure that if you offer me the job, I won't be walking into a disaster. I don't mind long odds, but I don't want impossible odds," he responded.

Sensing her confusion, Steve smiled quickly, his considerable charm in evidence. "I'm sorry if it seems like I'm just lobbing the ball back into your court, Cynthia. But from what you've told me about your own experience, I trust you to make the right call. I really do."

Should Cynthia Hire Steve?

Five commentators offer expert advice.

➤ David A. Thomas

David A. Thomas is the H. Naylor Fitzhugh Professor of Business Administration at Harvard Business School in Boston.

I am often surprised by managers' assumptions that their clients are not as good or as decent as they are: "I might be willing to accept a very talented person of color, but I don't believe my clients are ready for that yet.

And I'm not willing to risk finding out if I'm wrong." Their assumptions become self-fulfilling prophecies.

Peter Jones is making that kind of assumption. He comes right out and advises Cynthia Mitchell not to hire Steve Ripley. This doesn't happen as much as it used to; what's more likely to happen today is that, when Cynthia goes to Peter, he doesn't convey as clearly as he could that she shouldn't hire Steve. He equivocates instead, and Steve usually gets the job. Then when the first sign of difficulty arises, everybody bails. They say, "I knew this wasn't going to work," and not much energy gets invested in helping Steve succeed. At best, people go into sympathy mode. Everybody speaks with an understanding voice, but nobody says, "Let me mentor you. Let's see what sales tactics you're using. Let's talk you up to the clients."

Assuming that Cynthia offers Steve the job—which she should—here's what should happen. First, Cynthia does her homework. She gets a clear sense of who the clients are. Then she sets Steve up with a very good list of prospects. This will resonate with clients; people know when they've been put on a list of "desirables." They will assume that Cynthia wouldn't send a rep who would underserve the best clients, and they will be more open to Steve as a result.

Second, Cynthia has to be unequivocal in her support of Steve. When I researched the career paths of successful minority professionals, many of them described a pivotal moment when they started to believe they would succeed. It often happened when a client resisted being served by them—and their managers didn't hesitate to counter with,

"This is our best person." That kind of support may be the most important thing Cynthia can give Steve.

Cynthia needs to see herself as Steve's sponsor. That means working with Steve, but it also means working with other people to communicate her high expectations for him. She has to let the other sales reps know that he's excellent; if they get that message, they'll reach out to him and include him in their informal networks.

She also needs to help him read signals. It's not unusual for someone's social clock to be a little off when he or she is just starting out. Maybe Steve gets invited to an event and he passes, thinking it's not important—but it is. His absence gets interpreted in a negative way, because everyone assumes he understood. It's essential that Cynthia help him navigate these situations, because this is a company with very low expectations for black success.

Steve, in turn, has to understand that he needs Cynthia. He probably underestimates the degree to which the cards are stacked against him. He knows he's good, he knows he has great credentials—why wouldn't he succeed? But if things aren't working out, he needs to get on it fast, and he needs Cynthia to help him sort out the problems.

If I were Steve, I would figure out what an exceptionally successful rep looks like after one year and measure myself against that. If everyone is treating me well, but somehow it's not translating into the right performance metrics, then I need to start having conversations. Steve also needs to find the African-Americans who have succeeded at

AgFunds. (Cynthia should help him.) He should ask for their help and find out what their districts look like. (I bet their districts look a lot like this one.) Somehow those individuals were able to defy the negative predictions; Steve may find someone with enough self-awareness to tell him how it happened.

➤ Herman Morris, Jr.

Herman Morris, Jr., is the president and CEO of Memphis Light, Gas & Water Division in Tennessee.

Cynthia's problem isn't an uncommon one. I've placed young men and women in regions that were racially insular, knowing that they would need a lot of support to succeed, and I've certainly encountered resistance in my own career. So I'm fully aware of both sides' risks.

Cynthia ought to offer Steve the job. He's got the qualities she's looking for, and he's the top choice. To allow discriminatory customers to prevent Cynthia from making an offer to the best-qualified candidate is, well, it's just plain wrong. (It also puts the company at risk for a discrimination claim—one, I believe, with considerable merit.)

When Cynthia makes the offer to Steve, she should do so judiciously. She needs to be, as she apparently is, up-front and direct. Tell him it's likely to be a tough first assignment. Assure him that she'll support him, even if the odds seem overwhelming at times. AgFunds will be asking

Steve to accept significant risk, and I think it's reasonable to assure him that he'll get a second chance if this one doesn't pan out.

Cynthia herself has a huge challenge. She needs to turn around a district that's been losing customers for 15 years. That's not going to happen right away. But there could be a silver lining for both Cynthia and Steve. Some prospective customers in the district will be hungry for strong performance. If they find it's forthcoming, they might let that factor, rather than race or gender, drive their business decisions. Performance could be the great equalizer here.

Peter and the other district managers need to take a long look in the mirror. Peter says he wants to see Steve's career get off to a good start, but his paternalism is suspect and a bit offensive. There's no indication that AgFunds has attempted to reform customers' attitudes or to mentor and support the previous minority representatives. And Peter's concern about showing favoritism to Steve rings hollow when you consider that Cynthia's predecessor as district manager was allowed to perform poorly for 15 years before being called to account.

The silence of the other district managers suggests that they know Peter's not going to support Steve. It seems to me that this whole group is passively watching a talented young person's career wither and die on the vine. This affirmative inaction is pernicious. It denies Steve the opportunity to succeed, to fail, to try, or to find out why. It also denies AgFunds an opportunity to recover its investment in him.

Should Steve accept the job? Well, right now his career is stalled. He was first in his class, yet he's the last to find a position. Most of the managers in the region presume that he'll fail because of factors that aren't his fault. If he

---

It seems to me that this whole group is passively watching a talented young person's career wither and die on the vine. This affirmative inaction is pernicious.

---

doesn't fail—if he helps Cynthia turn around this difficult district—then his career prospects within the company will be very positive indeed. So I'd advise him to get assurances from Cynthia about support and future opportunities—and then to accept the job.

Cynthia, in turn, needs to work very closely with Steve. Given the underperformance of the incumbent sales staff, she should be the one to show Steve the ropes. Beyond that day-to-day coaching, Steve will undoubtedly need Cynthia to stand up for him on occasion. In my first job as a lawyer, if a customer had any concerns because of my race, he or she got a very strong message from the senior partners: "You retained the firm; every one of our lawyers is excellent and enjoys the full support of the firm." Steve's going to need that kind of support from time to time. If he gets it, he has a good shot at long-term success.

➤ Daryl Koehn and Alicia Leung

Daryl Koehn is the director of the Center for Business Ethics at the University of St. Thomas in Houston. Alicia Leung is an assistant professor of management at Hong Kong Baptist University. Koehn and Leung have collaborated on research examining the ethical problems that arise during cross-cultural interactions.

Cynthia is right to feel uncomfortable with Peter's reasoning. Peter is forgetting that Steve has advanced this far by dint of persistence and determination. No doubt he has faced discrimination in the past and has devised strategies for coping. The Arkansas market appears to be a tough one, but Steve may actually be better suited than other AgFunds sales representatives to crack it: Some studies have shown that minorities, who are accustomed to being treated as outsiders, often outperform other groups in stressful or difficult situations. If Cynthia thinks Steve is the right person for the job, she should offer it to him. She should make sure, however, that management establishes reasonable sales goals for this territory. No one is going to turn this market around overnight.

Peter is on dangerous ground when he imputes racial bias to all Arkansas farmers. What he sees as racial bias may simply be agrarian conservatism or a rural suspicion of city folk. Accustomed to working by themselves, farmers can be rather taciturn, but Steve's charm and quick wit may enable him to draw them out. Even if these potential customers are prejudiced, people can be won over. Ethnic Chinese living outside of China, Hong Kong, and Taiwan have long been discriminated against by local nationals, yet they are among the most successful businesspeople in the world.

Many multinational corporations face this same scenario. For years, white male executives have argued that women employees should not be given international postings because local nationals do not like to deal with female expatriates. Yet numerous studies have shown that these women have had managerial success in Japan, Korea, and the Middle East—regions characterized (by white males) as hostile to women. Women tend to be better at learning the indirect style preferred in many parts of the world. And they tend to nurture personal relationships more successfully, thereby gaining greater access than their white male peers to senior business contacts. Peter assumes that Steve's racial and cultural differences will be a problem. Sometimes, though, diversity is an aid, not an obstacle, to developing rapport.

Indeed, Asians and Europeans often perceive white American males as arrogant, impatient, blunt, and insensitive to cultural differences and nuances. Yet Peter probably would not think twice about sending a white male employee to a foreign posting. This case is as much about

Peter's biases and preconceptions as it is about supposed prejudices in Arkansas.

Imputing racial bias to customers in Arkansas sounds like an attempt by senior managers at AgFunds to deflect blame from themselves. Business executives often blame their own poor performance on extraneous factors—the September 11 attacks, the economic downturn in Asia, the millennium computer bug. The truth is, the Arkansas market has been declining for 15 years, in part because senior executives failed to remove a nonperforming manager. Rather than obsess about whether Steve should be assigned to the Arkansas position, AgFunds should evaluate its overall personnel review system, its advertising and marketing strategies, and the products being offered in the faltering Arkansas market. And instead of waiting for the "right" job for Steve to materialize, the company should be creating opportunities for all employees.

AgFunds appears to have two job tracks—a fast track for white males and a low-profile track for women and minorities. If the company does not start thinking more creatively about its people, markets, and products, talented employees like Steve and Cynthia will move to more savvy competitors.

➤ Glenn C. Loury

Glenn C. Loury is a professor of economics at Boston University and the founding director of the university's Institute on Race and Social Division.

Forgive me, but as an economist, I look at this as a societal problem, not just one that affects individuals or organizations. Sometimes what's best for society isn't necessarily what's best for the individual players.

I can certainly see why this job candidate might be tempted to swallow his pride and say, "Let's move on." It's a high-risk assignment, and he's well within his rights to say, "No thanks." It might even be the smartest thing to do from his point of view. Similarly, I can see why the managers in the company might shy away from offering him the job. They believe that by putting Steve into this job, they'll jeopardize profits and further alienate customers who aren't very happy to begin with. They also believe it'll lower their success rate with minority employees. I don't see how we can blame them for caring about those performance measures; it's their job to pay attention to them.

But if the company maintains its reluctance to assign Steve to the job, and if Steve decides to walk away—both decisions made for perfectly good reasons—then a serious societal problem isn't getting addressed.

If the other sales reps didn't want to work with Steve, the company would have leverage over those employees. They could coach the problem employees; they could fire them if need be. If middle managers consistently failed to promote minority candidates, that's an issue higher management could fix, too. But if the problem lies with the customers' attitudes toward AgFunds' sales reps, the company has no legal recourse, and there isn't much leverage it can bring to bear. That's what makes this case interesting. You can't sue your customers.

But I wouldn't just say, "Take the path of least resistance and hire someone else." If Cynthia does that, she is letting the customers call the shots—and letting them perpetuate some pretty antiquated ideas about race. We all have an obligation to think about what's right as well as what's effective. And I don't think it's utopian or naïve to say that if a lot of people put up a little resistance, things can change.

Are we really sure this guy would fail? We don't know a lot about how he presents himself. I can imagine that an urban black man—somebody whose dress, speech, body language, and style all conformed to an urban black stereotype—would have serious trouble in this district. But imagine that Steve grew up on military bases all over the world and learned how to fit in anywhere. Maybe he's the kind of guy who can drink the right kind of beer, become interested in the right sports, make the right kind of small talk. Cynthia and Peter need to keep those sorts of distinctions in mind and make their judgments based on what this particular guy is like, aside from his skin color. Maybe Steve can win the farmers over; I doubt they're all bad people.

Assuming Steve has a shot at fitting in and making a place for himself, there's still a real risk involved for him. I wonder—is there no way to insulate him from damage? I understand that in a lot of businesses, the people who make it to the top are on a very clear path; they've experienced success after success after success. Maybe AgFunds is like that, and poor performance in an early assignment means you'll never climb very high. But these are some-what extraordinary circumstances, after all. Doesn't the company owe Steve some kind of assurance that it won't be a career killer if he does take this job? If he's a good cultural fit, Cynthia should give Steve a shot, but she should also offer him a lot of support, including a sense that he has a future with the company even if this particular assignment doesn't work out.

Originally published in July 2002

Reprint R0207A

DIANE L. COUTU

Losing It

Executive Summary

"It's worse than I thought. . . . She's completely lost her mind," says Harry Beecham, the CEO of blue chip management consultancy Pierce and Company. The perplexed executive was in a hotel suite with his wife in Amsterdam, the latest stop on his regular trek to dozens of Pierce offices worldwide. In his hand was a sheaf of paper—the same message sent over and over again by his star employee and protégée Katharina Waldburg. The end of the world is coming, she warned. "Someone is going to die."

Harry wouldn't have expected this sort of behavior from Katharina. After graduating with distinction from Oxford, she made a name for herself by

149

single-handedly building Pierce's organizational behavior practice. At 27, she's poised to become the youngest partner ever elected at the firm.

But Harry can't ignore the faxes in his hand. Or the stream-of-consciousness e-mails Katharina's been sending to one of the directors in Pierce's Berlin office—mostly gibberish but potentially disastrous to Katharina's reputation if they ever got out. Harry also can't dismiss reports from Roland Fuoroli, manager of the Berlin office, of a vicious verbal exchange Katharina had with him, or of an "over the top" lunch date Katharina had with one of Pierce's clients in which she was explaining the alphabet's role in the creation of the universe.

Harry is planning to talk to Katharina when he gets to Berlin. What should he say? And will it be too late? Four commentators offer their advice in this fictional case study. They are Kay Redfield Jamison, a professor of psychiatry and a coauthor of *Manic-Depressive Illness*; David E. Meen, a former director at McKinsey & Company; Norman Pearlstine, the editor in chief at Time Incorporated; and Richard Primus, an assistant law professor at the University of Michigan.

Harry Beecham seldom got more than five hours of sleep a night. That was part of the price he paid to be the managing director of Pierce and Company, a blue chip management consulting firm based in Manhattan, with offices in 42 countries and two more on the way. In the last month alone, Harry had traveled the company's global network—from Houston and Chicago to London, Berlin, and Istanbul, and then on to Beijing and Singapore. This evening he was back in London again for just one night.

Jet-lagged and badly in need of rest, Harry had gone to bed about ten, asking the front desk at the Savoy to hold all calls. An hour later his cell phone rang. "Who the hell?" he groused, as he rolled over and turned on the light.

"Harry? It's Karl." Karl von Schwerin was one of the directors in Pierce's Berlin office and a close friend of Harry's. The two men golfed together at St. Andrews whenever they got the opportunity, and they were godparents to each other's children. "I know I've probably woken you up, and I'm sorry, but I've been getting a bunch of really crazy e-mails from Katharina. I think something's seriously wrong."

Katharina Waldburg was Pierce's hottest young consultant and Harry's protégée. They had met nine years ago when Katharina was a freshman at Oxford University. She had written him a letter daring him to hire her as a summer intern. Impressed by her chutzpah, Harry decided to accept the challenge, and Katharina quickly established herself as a smart and creative young consultant. A couple of years later, when the American graduated with a congratulatory first from Oxford—taking the George Humphrey Prize for best overall performance by an undergraduate in psychology—Harry offered her a position as a first-year associate at Pierce.

The decision had been a no-brainer. To Harry, Katharina was more than a topflight thinker; she was an original. He just knew she would emerge as a star among the fiery young turks he was hiring to bring Pierce into the twenty-first century. So far Katharina had more than fulfilled her promise. In a company with a strong bias toward operations and finance, she had almost single-handedly built a thriving practice in organizational behavior. She brought to bear a deep knowledge of her field and had a gift for making CEOs aspire to be servant leaders—though she was by no means sentimental about leadership. There was always a counterintuitive edge to her ideas that made clients give Pierce a second look. So it was not surprising that at 27, Katharina was poised to become the youngest partner ever elected at Pierce and Company.

"Well, what do the e-mail messages say?" Harry asked, trying to rub the sleep from his eyes.

"That's the problem; they're mostly gibberish." Karl reported. "They're full of stream-of-consciousness stuff that just doesn't stop. One of them's about how *not* to solve the Riemann hypothesis, whatever that is. Another's a four-pager on how women in organizations are treated like prostitutes. I tell you, Harry, Katharina's not herself. If e-mails like this get out, she could destroy her reputation. We've got to do something fast."

Harry winced. This was the last thing he needed to hear right now. "I have a client meeting in Amsterdam tomorrow, Karl, and then I'm meeting Caroline. I just don't have time to think about this. You're close friends with Katharina—give her a call, and find out what the problem is. Tell her to take a few days off. I'll be back in Berlin at the end of the week, and I'll talk to her myself then."

The Confrontation

At 3:30 AM, Berlin time, Katharina Waldburg was wide awake. She had been wide awake for days—ever since Hugh, her poet boyfriend, unceremoniously dumped her for a dumb Swiss blonde. But Katharina wasn't upset. It wasn't her way to brood on disappointments.

She knew exactly what to do in these circumstances: dust herself off and move on.

Despite the time, Katharina showered and headed off to work. She jumped into the red BMW convertible her father had given her after her last big promotion at Pierce. Pushing 130 kilometers per hour, her long, wet hair blowing in the wind, Katharina felt a kind of film-star gaiety as she rode through the construction-ridden streets. Even at four in the morning, Berlin seemed irrepressibly alive. People were arguing in Ku'damm cafés, while bearded kids roamed the boulevards wearing T-shirts blaming America for the next world war. According to her watch, Katharina pulled into the office garage at precisely 4:22 AM. (Weird—that was the exact hour and minute she was born!) She took the elevator up to the ninth floor and bounded through the glass doors.

Inside the Pierce suite, Katharina flicked on the lights and headed for her office, where she turned on the computer and sat down to write. Words and ideas flowed from her mind as they never had before. She wrote about a subject that had become increasingly dear to her heart—the obsolescence of language. She wrote about the uncomfortable reality that people feel things, and their irrational feelings influence their economic choices. Elated, she felt sure her ideas would change the world.

Katharina was focused so intensely on her thoughts that she didn't hear Roland Fuoroli enter her office at

7:30 that morning. Roland managed the Berlin office and was Katharina's immediate boss. He was also one of the firm's most accomplished directors in corporate cost cutting. Most of the time, Roland and Katharina didn't see eye to eye. For one thing, Roland was the consummate politician, and politics was a skill Katharina grossly underestimated. For another, Roland made no bones about his disregard for Pierce's organizational-behavior practice. Roland was into facts; he didn't have much tolerance for the "soft crap." Normally, Katharina was almost too conciliatory to Roland in their interactions, but today she felt uninhibited.

"So what do you want?" she asked with agitation when she noticed Roland.

"I was just wondering what you're working on," he explained, urbane as usual. "You've been holed up here for a week, and I'm trying to figure out how I can help."

"*You* help *me*?" Katharina barked, laughing out loud. "I don't need any help from you."

"Now, Katharina," Roland responded smoothly, "don't be abrasive."

"Abrasive?" she countered. "You know what, Roland? I may be abrasive, but you are mediocre. And I can always go to charm school, but you will always be mediocre."

Roland's eyebrows shot up, and the two locked eyes for a full minute before he responded. "Katharina," he said, speaking slowly and distinctly, "I don't know what this is all about, but I will not accept this kind of verbal assault. You are being disrespectful, and if you continue like this, you will never become a partner."

Katharina paused for effect. "Oh really," she drawled, "And how do you spell lawsuit? Because if I were a man, my abrasive style would never even be an issue."

Roland walked away, training his gaze on a crack in the floor as he moved out of the room. Katharina's attack on him had been vicious, and he had wondered for a fleeting moment if she would attack him physically. "We've got a nasty situation on our hands," he said, talking to nobody in particular.

The Awakening

After her fight with Roland, Katharina went home to continue her frenzied writing in private. An hour of animated typing passed, and Katharina's mind suddenly seemed to clear. She felt that she understood exactly what to do. It was a plan she absolutely had to share, and she knew just who to share it with: José Müller. She rang his office. Fortunately, he was in, and the two friends arranged to meet for lunch at the Borchardt at one.

Katharina and José often lunched together—they loved to gossip about the business world's movers and shakers. At 59, José was the chairman and CEO of

Mitska AG, one of the largest retail chains in Europe, headquartered in Berlin. The son of a Spanish flamenco dancer and a German businessman, José was as irreverent and entrepreneurial as he was no-nonsense. He also had more business savvy than anyone Katharina knew. Over the past 30 years, he had transformed a conservative, family-owned department store in West Germany into an international chain of low-cost retail outlets. When Mitska went public in 1992, José became one of the richest men in Europe. He was not Katharina's client—Roland had the business relationship with him—but José and Katharina had met at a Pierce function and immediately hit it off. José liked Katharina. He thought she was vivacious and funny and that, like him, she had a fierce desire to compete.

Katharina was not surprised to see that José was already waiting for her when she got to the restaurant. He pulled out her chair as the waiter brought their menus. Katharina was in high spirits, and her expansiveness was catching. José ordered a bottle of wine, and the two of them laughed and drank until Katharina got down to business. "Look, José," she said, flush with enthusiasm, "I've been giving this a lot of thought, and I think your company could use a shrink incentive plan. You can transform your entire profitability by encouraging high performers to get the help they need." Katharina stopped and hunched forward, waiting for a reaction.

José was bewildered. "Hey, slow down. I'm not following you. Are we talking about shrinkage here? Theft? Unaccounted inventory loss?"

"Oh, José!" Katharina exclaimed, getting impatient, "you've got to listen faster. I'm talking about psychological loss, not physical loss. I'm talking about losses so severe that maybe nothing can ever make them right again. Smart people, people who have everything going for them—even people like you and me—sometimes need shrinks to help them grieve. Otherwise, they can't focus on their work. If you think about it a bit, you'll agree that my idea is not as strange as it sounds."

José sat back in his chair and laughed. "Katharina, that's the most ridiculous idea I've ever heard. Retailers don't need shrinks; I certainly don't want one. Anyway, therapy has always seemed like a lot of hocus-pocus to me."

Katharina broke into tears. José was taken aback, confused by her outburst. "Look, Katharina, I'm not a psychological guy. You must have figured that out by now. So what is this, some kind of joke? You laugh, you cry, you come up with some harebrained scheme about a shrink incentive plan. Are you pulling my leg?"

"Forget it," Katharina replied. "It's not really what I wanted to talk to you about anyway. There's something more important I need to discuss." In a flash, her mood had changed. She looked at him intently, her eyes glittering.

"José, I'm seeing signs everywhere. I mean, you take a city like Berlin. The Allies divided it on September 12, and September 12 is my birthday. And John and Jackie Kennedy were married on September 12, and then President Kennedy comes to Berlin and says '*Ich bin ein Berliner.*' And now I am a Berliner. For the first time in my life, I feel like I'm seeing the connections that underlie all things."

José had no idea what Katharina was on about. Nervously, he hedged. "Katharina, I think you'll find coincidences if you look for them. But they're just random events."

"José, I'm seeing signs everywhere ...
I can't prove it, but I am totally
and utterly convinced that
God created the world by giving
the universe a letter."

"I am not just making things up," Katharina retorted, her voice shaking and her fists now clenched. "I tell you, I'm getting all kinds of messages—revelations, if you like." She leaned in and lowered her voice. "You know, I can't prove it, but I am totally and utterly convinced that God created the world by giving the universe a letter."

José looked at Katharina incredulously. He sincerely wasn't sure whether she was having a breakdown or a breakthrough, but he knew he didn't want to upset her again. "All right" he said, "so tell me then. What letter did God create the world with?"

"Oh, probably *i*," Katharina said gleefully, and then she started to laugh so violently that she almost fell off her chair. "Or maybe it's *u*! Maybe *u* is God's gift to the world!"

José wiped his mouth with his napkin and took Katharina's arm. "Come on," he said, embarrassed. "You've definitely had too much to drink; it's time for you to go home."

The Apocalypse

Katharina didn't know how she had gotten home after her lunch with José. Her consciousness drifted between waves of reality and unreality, and she couldn't remember anything until she found herself staring at the insides of her empty oven. In the living room, the television was blaring. Katharina tried to ignore it as she listened to her voice mails. Karl had called six or seven times, asking her to call him back. Roland had left an angry message. He said he had been talking to José, who told him that Katharina was coming unglued.

Katharina pulled the telephone out of the wall; she couldn't face anyone right now. Feeling exposed and betrayed, she moved into the living room and plopped down on the couch. She switched the channel to ARD and began watching the evening news. It was gruesome, as usual. In Iraq, America's allies, military and civilian, were paying a deadly price for U.S. intervention in the region. Elsewhere in the Middle East, Israeli attacks on the West Bank and Gaza Strip had killed 15 more Palestinians, bringing the count to 422 deaths in the last 11 months alone. (4-2-2—the exact time she was born!) Suddenly, she had a moment of such utter terror that she felt as if she were frozen in free fall. That's when Katharina knew nuclear war was imminent—and that Berlin was going to be ground zero.

She realized she had to warn Harry of the impending apocalypse—and she had to warn him now. She promptly called his secretary in New York to find out where he was staying. Scribbling the fax number down on a scrap of paper—31 for Holland, and then 4159265—Katharina replaced the receiver and grabbed a can of Coke from the refrigerator. Gulping down the soda, she went to the computer where she sat down to write what she knew would probably be the most important letter of her career.

Dear Harry,
   You've probably heard about Roland and me by now. But I have to tell you, this is really an

organizational problem. You hire the smartest women you can find, and then you put us under men who are terrified of our intelligence. But Harry, I've got something more important to say. <u>PLEASE</u> listen to me. Everywhere I look I keep getting premonitions that the world is coming to an end. I saw that movie Z on television last night, the one about the politician who gets murdered. I have no grounds for it, but I feel quite certain that someone is going to die, though I don't know y. Does u? Oh, Harry, I wish I could explain how utterly petrified I am. Wouldn't it be lovely if u and i could just be together?

    K.

    (An angry woman)

Katharina finished her letter and faxed it to Harry in the Netherlands. To be sure he received it, she faxed him a second copy, and a third, and then, finally, Katharina felt she had done everything she could do. Wired and restless, she crawled into bed and put out the light. Wide awake, Katharina Waldburg was once again in the dark.

Judgment Day

At 9:11 PM the bellboy at Amsterdam's Bilderberg Garden Hotel paid a visit to Harry and his wife Caroline in their suite. He held several faxed pages in his hands. "I'm sorry to disturb you, sir, but the sender indicated that these were extremely urgent."

Harry skimmed Katharina's faxes and slumped back in his chair. "God, Caroline, it's worse than I thought. She's not just angry, she's mad. She's completely lost her mind."

Harry went to the suite bar and mixed a Manhattan for his wife and a martini for himself. As they sipped their drinks, Harry reflected on recent events and tried to put them together logically in his mind.

He knew a little something about these things; he had a wildly talented aunt who ended up in an asylum after she tried to buy Bogotá. But with Katharina it had all happened so fast. Until a few days ago, she was one of Pierce's best consultants. She had been talking to clients about the benefits of practical paranoia, and in a country like Germany, where executives were desperate to regain any competitive edge, her ideas about the paranoid organization had been a big hit.

But attacking Roland in the office and offending clients crossed the boundaries of what was acceptable.

"She's got to be stopped—for her own good and for the good of the company," Harry told Caroline, sounding definitive. "The question is, Should I cut her loose? That's what Roland wants. He's already told me that he won't stay if Katharina's gross infractions are overlooked and she makes partner. She went out and got drunk with his client. That's just not something we can tolerate. But if we fire her, we could end up getting sued. And if we don't take care of Katharina, who will?"

Caroline nodded, recalling that Katharina's father, her only living relative, had died a few months ago. She sat down on the sofa beside Harry. "Maybe you can convince her to take a medical leave. Maybe that's all Katharina needs—a little time to get her feet back on the ground."

"That's not going to be easy," Harry said, shaking his head at the thought. "She is extremely independent. On the other hand, she's not in any position right now to decide what's best for herself. Caroline, you don't think I should try to have her hospitalized, do you? I mean, on what grounds could I do that? Sure, she showed poor judgment with Roland and José. And she sent around some oddball memos. But if I tried to hospitalize every associate who sent me rambling e-mails, the asylums would be full."

There didn't seem to be much more to say. Harry and Caroline sat in silence for a few minutes. Finally, Harry mused wearily: "You know, in some ways, I feel partly responsible. Three times Roland told me that he didn't want Katharina working in the Berlin office. He felt threatened by Katharina—I know that now—but she wanted to be in Berlin so badly that I persuaded him to take her. Maybe it was the tension between them that pushed her over the edge. She's so talented, I thought she could handle anything that came her way. Obviously there was some vulnerability there that I didn't see. I don't think Katharina saw it herself.

"Now she's going 200 miles an hour, and things can't wait until I get to Berlin on Friday. Katharina may try to get in touch with other clients or, worse, she could do something to hurt herself. What a mess. I honestly don't know what to do."

What Should Harry Do About Katharina?

Four commentators offer expert advice.

➤ Kay Redfield Jamison

Kay Redfield Jamison is a professor of psychiatry at the Johns Hopkins University School of Medicine in Baltimore. She is a coauthor of the classic medical textbook Manic-Depressive Illness *(Oxford University Press, 1990) and a John D. and Catherine T. MacArthur Fellow.*

The most important thing to know about this case is that Katharina Waldburg's probable condition—mania—is far from uncommon. On average, one person in 100 will suffer from manic depression (or bipolar illness, as it is also called) in the severe form described here, and another two or three will experience it in a milder form. In high-powered environments, such as the one at

Pierce and Company, the numbers will be even higher. In other words, a lot of businesspeople have bipolar illness, but because of the stigma involved, no one admits it, and the illness goes untreated.

This is regrettable because manic depression is a very treatable illness—science is clear on this.

A company can do several things to prepare itself for situations such as the one Harry Beecham faces—not the least of which is to develop general guidelines for handling psychiatric crises in the workplace. Businesses can specify the measures managers should take in cases like Katharina's. For instance, they can make sure their senior managers are educated about the symptoms of major mental illnesses.

I cannot emphasize strongly enough the value of having guidelines in place; in this day and age, there can be a big difference between what a CEO might *want* to do and what he *can* do legally.

The first consideration in dealing with a manic employee is to guarantee the individual's safety, as well as the safety of other people in the office. All exchanges and actions involving the person should be meticulously documented. That's important because situations like the one described in the case can end up in a courtroom; in addition to the usual legal concerns for a company when an employee is let go, litigiousness is a common symptom of mania. Good documentation affords the company some protection.

Companies should also be aware that mania can lead to reckless financial behavior; indeed, such recklessness is often considered to be an integral part of the illness. Harry needs to resolve this situation quickly to avert potential financial trouble.

Pierce may need to consider staging an intervention. That is, the company might want to try to persuade Katharina to confront the reality of her illness and acknowledge that she needs treatment. Interventions outside the workplace typically involve a group of people with close personal or social ties to the sufferer—for instance, family, friends, or members of the clergy. It may, however, be legally impossible for an employer to bring these people together; privacy and other sensitive issues may be raised if the employer tries. What Harry can do is bring together several of Katharina's colleagues who can try to help her seek out qualified medical advice and even hospitalization if necessary.

With ongoing treatment, most employees with bipolar illness *can* reenter the workforce. It may take Katharina a period of time to get well, but the odds are good that she will recover. One way Pierce can help Katharina is by simply reassuring her that she would be welcomed back once she has been successfully treated. Unfortunately, organizations often see individuals with psychiatric illness as untreatable, which can make it hard for them to regain acceptance once they have recovered. In my experience, even medical schools, which you might think would be understanding about mental illness, can be quite punitive in this respect.

Here, as in the business world, basic education about the symptoms and treatability of mania and depression is invaluable.

➤ David E. Meen

Until June 2003, David E. Meen was a director of McKinsey & Company. He was an office manager for more than 17 years at several McKinsey locations including Canada, Brussels, and Turkey. He can be reached at davidmeen@M-part.com.

Reading this case gave me a brief but sobering insight into the horror of manic depression—though how can you really know it unless you've lived it? Harry has to put aside legal and business considerations and simply respond to Katharina as a concerned human being reaching out to someone in distress. His star employee has no family; to my mind, that makes Harry morally responsible for her, at the very least.

In some ways, it may be easier for Harry to react this way than it would be for most CEOs. Consulting firms are relatively nonhierarchical organizations, and as the manager of such a company, Harry probably regards Katharina as a colleague in the fullest sense of that word. Call it mutual dependency, enlightened self-interest, or even a sense of extended family—people management is "up close and personal" in most professional services firms I'm familiar with. In fact, that's one of the career's main attractions. You get to work side by side with highly talented and motivated people who give you everything they have. Harry can't take all Katharina has to offer without fulfilling his commitment to her now that she needs him.

Even if Harry were the CEO of a public corporation, adopting a humane attitude would still be the right thing to do. When managers treat a distressed employee with respect and caring, they create enormous reservoirs of good-

---

Harry has to put aside legal and business considerations and simply respond to Katharina as a concerned human being reaching out to someone in distress.

---

will in their organizations. This shouldn't be the only reason for the CEO to respond humanely, but it's a reality that corporate managers often forget.

Given his own responsibilities to Pierce and to his other colleagues, Harry probably cannot commit the time that the situation demands, and he should find someone else to lead the intervention. Normally, that would be Katharina's office manager, but given her difficult relationship with Roland, involving him might well fuel her growing paranoia.

The right person is probably Karl von Schwerin, who has the advantage of being Katharina's friend. However, even as he asks Karl to take the lead (after consultation with Roland), Harry will want to stay close to the situation because he has a responsibility both to Katharina and to Pierce for ensuring that her crisis is well managed. He can't delegate the task and then wash his hands of it. Besides, Karl is floundering, as many managers would in this situation. When he got crazy e-mails from Katharina, his instinct was to run to Harry. It would have been more productive—and more professional—if he had spent some time trying to understand the nature and degree of Katharina's crisis.

Karl should talk to Katharina immediately to assess whether she is aware of the consequences of her actions. He should talk to her colleagues to see if they have any insight into her state of mind. Then he should find out whether she has a doctor or psychiatrist who can be notified. If there is such a professional in Katharina's life, Karl may want to seek that person's advice on how Pierce can best help Katharina. Obviously, the company could be entering a legal gray area with these inquiries, but Harry and Karl should not let those concerns inhibit their attempts to help a colleague in anguish.

Katharina will have to go on medical leave. In arranging that, Pierce should make it clear that she can come back when she gets better. If she does return, Katharina and Harry need to have some serious conversations about her future role. Could she resume the full-time life of a consultant? Or would the stress of that position exacerbate her vulnerabilities? What other positions could she take? There are many ways an extraordinarily talented individual like Katharina could add value to the company—but that's for another day. For now, Katharina needs Pierce's help, and Pierce needs to be there for her.

➤ Norman Pearlstine

Norman Pearlstine is the editor in chief of Time Incorporated in New York. He can be reached at Pearlstine@timeinc.com.

Few bosses facing Harry's dilemma are going to behave the same way. Despite all the packaged theories we have on management behavior, the reality is that leaders bring their upbringing and their personal experiences to the job, especially when they're faced with a new situation. That was true for me back in the early 1980s when I was the editor and publisher of the *Wall Street Journal Europe* and one of my journalists had a psychotic episode similar to Katharina's.

Today, I can see that there were personal reasons behind my decision to try and help this journalist. My family has a history of manic depression. My father was a brilliant, extraordinary lawyer with a 20-man practice outside of Philadelphia. In 1959, when I was 16, he went into deep depression, underwent electroshock therapy, and was hospitalized for three months. When he came out, he was taking lithium but nevertheless continued to have manic and depressed moods over many years. Although I didn't consciously think about him when my journalist began to exhibit similar problems, I do believe that my experiences with my father made me acutely aware that people in desperate mental distress need a reason for hope.

I also wanted to help because I felt that this particular journalist was one of the most gifted people I knew. I wanted her to succeed because I could see what she was capable of. That made sense even from a narrow corporate perspective. It is people like her and Katharina who come up with the breakthrough idea, the breakthrough story, the breakthrough technology that really distinguishes your organization from everybody else's. I felt that if we could just help this woman through her crisis, her potential to contribute to the organization could be very significant.

Of course, a corporation has fiduciary obligations to its owners, clients, and employees. If an employee's behavior becomes so disruptive that it affects other people's ability to work—or if it could put the company at risk—then that person has to be removed from the workplace. My own instincts are always to try to make things work, but when someone becomes really psychotic, as my journalist did, you have to accept that she needs professional help rather than managerial hand-holding.

So I encouraged her to take a medical leave, which she did. At the same time, I promised her that no matter how long it took her to recover, she would have a job at the *Journal* so long as I was there. The unstated and unwritten condition was that she had to be in shape to handle the work whenever she did return.

Both she and I moved on from the *Journal*, but she told me years later—and I have followed her subsequent and successful career with interest—that my promise to her was instrumental in her recovery. It goes without saying, of course, that the nature of the corporation affects what a manager can or cannot do in these situations. Managers of large organizations like Dow Jones or Time Warner can often do more to help because their companies have deep pockets.

When I faced a dilemma equivalent to Harry's, I relied largely on my instincts. Would I do anything different today? Perhaps not. For better and for worse, I am a person who is highly aware of how my decisions affect other people. That's not always a good thing, but it's who I am. In the past 20 years, though, I have learned to be cautious. In balancing the interests of the company against those of the employee, I would probably rely much more on the advice of professionals—attorneys, human resource people, and so forth. As much as I would like to avoid doing that, I would have very little choice in today's litigious society.

➤ Richard Primus

Richard Primus is an assistant law professor at the University of Michigan in Ann Arbor, where he teaches constitutional law and employment discrimination law. A Rhodes Scholar, he is the author of The American Language of Rights *(Cambridge, 1999).*

Katharina's crisis has certainly raised some legal questions for Pierce and Company, but there is no need for Harry to panic. Given the facts of the case, Pierce's exposure to legal action is probably quite limited.

Because Pierce is a U.S. corporation and Katharina an American citizen, Katharina's employment is subject to U.S. law. There are two possible grounds for an action by

Katharina against Pierce: sex discrimination and disability. The relevant legislation for sex discrimination is Title VII of the Civil Rights Act of 1964. An action on the basis of disability would be governed by the Americans with Disabilities Act of 1990.

Katharina told Roland she would sue Pierce if she were denied partnership for being abrasive. Under Title VII, which prohibits sex discrimination in the workplace, employers can't have different behavioral expectations for men and women. If it can be proved in court that Pierce accepts abrasive behavior from men but not from women, then Katharina has a good Title VII claim. But if Pierce can show that it treats abrasive men and women in the same way, then Katharina has no case for sex discrimination.

The disability issue is more complex. The ADA makes it illegal for companies to discriminate against employees because of a physical or mental disability. To gain ADA protection, Katharina must be a *qualified person with a disability*—words that have a very specific meaning under the ADA.

The ADA defines people as "disabled" if they have mental or physical defects that substantially limit "major life activities." These activities include obvious physical activities such as seeing, walking, and performing manual tasks, which Katharina can clearly do. However, working is also considered to be a major life activity, so if her condition prevents Katharina from doing her job and other jobs like it, she might be protected by the ADA. Her situation in this respect, however, is somewhat murky as she has not been diagnosed as having any particular defect.

The complication cuts deeper: Even if she were to be recognized legally as having a debilitating mental defect, Katharina might not turn out to be a *qualified* person. To be qualified, an employee has to be able to do her job given some reasonable accommodation. Assume that Katharina asks Pierce for a lighter workload. If she can function well under the new situation, she would be entitled to the protections of the ADA. But if she still can't do her work despite that reasonable accommodation, then the ADA doesn't protect her.

Pierce is not legally obliged to offer any accommodation unless Katharina asks for it; the company is entitled to fire her now. If Katharina sued, Pierce would have to be able to prove that the reason for dismissal was performance and not disability, which might be hard to establish given Katharina's record. It is therefore in Pierce's interests to work with Katharina to identify a reasonable accommodation. If Katharina accepts the accommodation and still performs badly, then Pierce can probably dismiss her without consequences. Even if Pierce fails to find an accommodation acceptable to Katharina, it will still have some protection because in that case Katharina's claim will be limited to the implementation of a reasonable accommodation as defined by the court. She will not be entitled to monetary damages. Only if Pierce hasn't tried to find a reasonable accommodation can Katharina sue for damages as well.

Originally published in April 2004

Reprint R0404A

ABOUT THE CONTRIBUTORS

Jeffrey C. Connor is a partner at Spectrum OED, a consulting firm in Brookline, Massachusetts, that specializes in organization and executive development. He is also the executive director of Seacoast Mental Health Center in Portsmouth, New Hampshire, and a lecturer on organizational behavior at Harvard Medical School.

Diane L. Coutu is a senior editor at *Harvard Business Review*, specializing in psychology and business. Her article "How Resilience Works" appeared in the May 2002 issue of *Harvard Business Review*.

Alden M. Hayashi is a former senior editor at *Harvard Business Review*.

John Humphreys, a former executive in the financial services industry, is an associate professor of management at the College of Business at Eastern New Mexico University in Portales.

Julia Kirby is a senior editor at *Harvard Business Review*.

Joan Magretta is a management consultant and writer and a past winner of *Harvard Business Review's* McKinsey Award.

Byron Reimus is a Philadelphia-based writer and consultant on workplace communication issues.

Harvard Business Review Paperback Series

The Harvard Business Review Paperback Series offers the best thinking on cutting-edge management ideas from the world's leading thinkers, researchers, and managers. Designed for leaders who believe in the power of ideas to change business, these books will be useful to managers at all levels of experience, but especially senior executives and general managers. In addition, this series is widely used in training and executive development programs.

Books are priced at US$19.95
Price subject to change.

Title	Product #
Harvard Business Review **Interviews with CEOs**	3294
Harvard Business Review on **Advances in Strategy**	8032
Harvard Business Review on **Appraising Employee Performance**	7685
Harvard Business Review on **Becoming a High Performance Manager**	1296
Harvard Business Review on **Brand Management**	1445
Harvard Business Review on **Breakthrough Leadership**	8059
Harvard Business Review on **Breakthrough Thinking**	181X
Harvard Business Review on **Building Personal and Organizational Resilience**	2721
Harvard Business Review on **Business and the Environment**	2336
Harvard Business Review on **The Business Value of IT**	9121
Harvard Business Review on **Change**	8842
Harvard Business Review on **Compensation**	701X
Harvard Business Review on **Corporate Ethics**	273X
Harvard Business Review on **Corporate Governance**	2379
Harvard Business Review on **Corporate Responsibility**	2748
Harvard Business Review on **Corporate Strategy**	1429
Harvard Business Review on **Crisis Management**	2352
Harvard Business Review on **Culture and Change**	8369
Harvard Business Review on **Customer Relationship Management**	6994

Title	Product #
Harvard Business Review on **Decision Making**	5572
Harvard Business Review on **Doing Business in China**	6387
Harvard Business Review on **Effective Communication**	1437
Harvard Business Review on **Entrepreneurship**	9105
Harvard Business Review on **Finding and Keeping the Best People**	5564
Harvard Business Review on **Innovation**	6145
Harvard Business Review on **The Innovative Enterprise**	130X
Harvard Business Review on **Knowledge Management**	8818
Harvard Business Review on **Leadership**	8834
Harvard Business Review on **Leadership at the Top**	2756
Harvard Business Review on **Leadership in a Changed World**	5011
Harvard Business Review on **Leading in Turbulent Times**	1806
Harvard Business Review on **Managing Diversity**	7001
Harvard Business Review on **Managing High-Tech Industries**	1828
Harvard Business Review on **Managing People**	9075
Harvard Business Review on **Managing Projects**	6395
Harvard Business Review on **Managing the Value Chain**	2344
Harvard Business Review on **Managing Uncertainty**	9083
Harvard Business Review on **Managing Your Career**	1318
Harvard Business Review on **Marketing**	8040
Harvard Business Review on **Measuring Corporate Performance**	8826
Harvard Business Review on **Mergers and Acquisitions**	5556
Harvard Business Review on **Mind of the Leader**	6409
Harvard Business Review on **Motivating People**	1326
Harvard Business Review on **Negotiation**	2360
Harvard Business Review on **Nonprofits**	9091
Harvard Business Review on **Organizational Learning**	6153
Harvard Business Review on **Strategic Alliances**	1334
Harvard Business Review on **Strategies for Growth**	8850
Harvard Business Review on **Turnarounds**	6366
Harvard Business Review on **What Makes a Leader**	6374
Harvard Business Review on **Work and Life Balance**	3286

Management Dilemmas:
Case Studies from the Pages of
Harvard Business Review

When facing a difficult management challenge, wouldn't it be great if you could turn to a panel of experts to help guide you to the right decision? Now you can, with books from the Management Dilemmas series. Drawn from the pages of *Harvard Business Review*, each insightful guide poses a range of familiar and perplexing business situations and shares the wisdom of a small group of leading experts on how each of them would resolve the problem. Engagingly written, these interactive, solutions-oriented collections allow readers to match wits with the experts. They are designed to help managers hone their instincts and problem-solving skills to make sound judgment calls on everyday management dilemmas.

These books are priced at US$19.95
Price subject to change.

Title	Product #
Management Dilemmas: **When Change Comes Undone**	5038
Management Dilemmas: **When Good People Behave Badly**	5046
Management Dilemmas: **When Marketing Becomes a Minefield**	290X
Management Dilemmas: **When People Are the Problem**	7138
Management Dilemmas: **When Your Strategy Stalls**	712X

Harvard Business Essentials

In the fast-paced world of business today, everyone needs a personal resource—a place to go for advice, coaching, background information, or answers. The Harvard Business Essentials series fits the bill. Concise and straightforward, these books provide highly practical advice for readers at all levels of experience. Whether you are a new manager interested in expanding your skills or an experienced executive looking to stay on top, these solution-oriented books give you the reliable tips and tools you need to improve your performance and get the job done. Harvard Business Essentials titles will quickly become your constant companions and trusted guides.

These books are priced at US$19.95, except as noted.
Price subject to change.

Title	Product #
Harvard Business Essentials: **Negotiation**	1113
Harvard Business Essentials: **Managing Creativity and Innovation**	1121
Harvard Business Essentials: **Managing Change and Transition**	8741
Harvard Business Essentials: **Hiring and Keeping the Best People**	875X
Harvard Business Essentials: **Finance**	8768
Harvard Business Essentials: **Business Communication**	113X
Harvard Business Essentials: **Manager's Toolkit ($24.95)**	2896
Harvard Business Essentials: **Managing Projects Large and Small**	3213
Harvard Business Essentials: **Creating Teams with an Edge**	290X
Harvard Business Essentials: **Entrepreneur's Toolkit**	4368
Harvard Business Essentials: **Coaching and Mentoring**	435X
Harvard Business Essentials: **Crisis Management**	4376

The Results-Driven Manager

The Results-Driven Manager series collects timely articles from *Harvard Management Update* and *Harvard Management Communication Letter* to help senior to middle managers sharpen their skills, increase their effectiveness, and gain a competitive edge. Presented in a concise, accessible format to save managers valuable time, these books offer authoritative insights and techniques for improving job performance and achieving immediate results.

These books are priced at US$14.95
Price subject to change.

Title	Product #
The Results-Driven Manager:	
Face-to-Face Communications for Clarity and Impact	3477
The Results-Driven Manager:	
Managing Yourself for the Career You Want	3469
The Results-Driven Manager:	
Presentations That Persuade and Motivate	3493
The Results-Driven Manager: **Teams That Click**	3507
The Results-Driven Manager:	
Winning Negotiations That Preserve Relationships	3485
The Results-Driven Manager: **Dealing with Difficult People**	6344
The Results-Driven Manager: **Taking Control of Your Time**	6352
The Results-Driven Manager: **Getting People on Board**	6360

How to Order

Harvard Business School Press publications are available worldwide
from your local bookseller or online retailer.
You can also call

1-800-668-6780

Our product consultants are available to help you
8:00 a.m.–6:00 p.m., Monday–Friday, Eastern Time.
Outside the U.S. and Canada, call: 617-783-7450
Please call about special discounts for quantities greater than ten.

You can order online at

www.HBSPress.org